Rea McDo

Prayer Pilgrimage
With Paul

Resources for Personal
and Small Group Prayer

Paulist Press
New York • Mahwah

Photo Credits

Chapter 1	Mia et Klaus
Chapter 2	Rick Smolan
Chapter 3	Mimi Forsyth
Chapter 4	Paul M. Schrock
Chapter 5	Mia et Klaus
Chapter 6	Mimi Forsyth

Library of Congress
Catalog Card Number: 85-61750

ISBN: 0-8091-2746-6

Published by Paulist Press
997 Macarthur Blvd.
Mahwah, N.J. 07430

Printed and bound in the United States of America

Contents

Dedicated to

**my Mother and Father,
to Jack, Joan, Joe and Chuck**

with whom I argued Paul forever

Acknowledgements

My deepest thanks to the woman who invited me to probe Paul with her many years ago, Margred Ulmer, S.S.N.D., and to the man who taught me most about prayer, Bob Doherty, S.J. Thanks to my current "group" with whom I can always share Scripture, prayer, Spirit, sin, grace, myself: Mary Irving, S.S.N.D., Rachel Callahan, C.S.C. and Nancy Steckel. Thanks to all who read the manuscript, and to Janet Sidor and Janet Knott who prepared it. Special gratitude to Norine and Lou Migliorini who turned over their oceanfront condominium to me for writing.

Introduction

I begin this book at the ocean in Rockport, Massachusetts. It is foggy, even misty, and the tide draws back. Seaweed covers the exposed rocks, and living barnacles along with their dead ancestors cling to the rocks. An image of our search for Paul. We always see through a glass darkly, through a mist, a fog, when we search the Scriptures. We search for God's own self in this book, God as revealed in Paul's experience. Parts of Paul's writings are living, breathing, still fastened to the Rock who is Christ; parts of his letters are shells empty of meaning for Christians living in the twentieth century, but held to the Rock by an historical rootedness that calls for our reverence.

As in my first book, *Prayer Pilgrimage Through Scripture*, I write with reverence, with the hope that my readers will be able to make a home in the word of God, may find themselves more comfortable in reading and praying with the letters of Paul. In a sense, that was Paul's hope too when he preached from the Jewish Scriptures and his own experience of the risen Christ, and when later he wrote to his communities. He wanted people to discover life in the Scriptures, life that was Christ Jesus himself, life that was the Spirit of the risen Lord. Jesus in John's Gospel promises us that if we make the word

1

our home we will be Jesus' disciples (learners), we will know the truth and the truth will set us free (Jn 8:32).

Paul has been called the apostle of freedom. That was his experience of the risen Lord, one who set him free. It is his experience of being freed in Christ Jesus, in the power of the Spirit which makes Paul an important dialogue partner in our own search for a deeper relationship with Christ, in Christ. That relationship we call prayer.

This is not primarily a book about Paul or his communities or about the literary form of ancient letters or about Paul's theology. Of course we have to read, study, and pray with Paul in context. This book, however, is primarily a prayer pilgrimage with a man who wrote: "Pray always, unceasingly" (1 Thes 5:17). What was Paul's own prayer like? his relationship with God? Jesus? the Spirit? Can Paul help us pray always or has he simply overstated his case as he so often does?

Hopefully, we will not search Paul's letters to find out why, how, when we should pray, relate with God, respond to God's faithful love. Rather we will first examine our own experience of prayer and then look to Paul's experience. We will put our relationship with God into dialogue with Paul's to see what in Paul's relationship affirms our experience and what can stretch and challenge our prayer.

We, hopefully, can live our life with God freely, uniquely, yet see it reflected in Paul. We do not want to use Paul's teaching and experience as a new law, a new norm to measure our spiritual progress. Thus I will only devote one chapter to the man himself but five chapters to our contemporary experience of Jesus, sin and reconciliation, the Spirit, the Church, and the gifts we have all received. I hope that then Paul's teachings which guided various communities in the first centuries might illumine our own relationships with Jesus and each other in our families and communities of today.

Using This Book

Each chapter will focus some questions first on you, the reader as individual and as member of a group. For example:

- What is your experience of Jesus—you, individually?
- How does (did) your family experience Jesus?
- What groups have fostered your experience of Jesus?
- What has been the experience of Jesus in your parish, diocese, country, worldwide denomination?

Then I will offer some brief commentary on Paul's experience of Jesus, salvation, the Spirit, the Church and our gifts. The comments are merely an introduction to the most important part of this book, the passages for prayer. This book is not meant to be read so much as to be used for letting the Spirit lead you to prayer, lead you in prayer as you ponder the words of Paul, the words of Scripture. After you take time for personal prayer, I hope that you can find or create a group for faith-sharing, simply stating what God revealed to you and in you, what you learned, how you became more a disciple, how your heart was moved when you prayed. Besides faith-sharing, other kinds of group activity can deepen the hold that the word has on you; I will offer suggestions for such activities and discussions. Finally, I will suggest further readings.

Praying

Before we begin our prayer pilgrimage, I would like to offer a working description of what I mean by prayer. Prayer is being in relationship with God, one which God initiates. Prayer is responding to God's initiative, bringing yourself to the Lord just as you are anytime, anywhere, in the midst of joy, pain, tenderness, anger, wonder, sin. Prayer is basically the activity of the Spirit within us, calling out to God, crying with "unutterable groanings" those desires we cannot even articulate (Rom 8:26). The Spirit, of course, prays constantly within us, even when we sleep. Our conscious time for prayer is like tuning in to the Spirit's prayer—just as the room you are sitting in now is full of radio waves but unless you tune in the radio, you are not aware of all the sound around you. Thus, there is no such thing as a "bad" prayer. If we are angry with God, we are offering our very real selves; if we are distracted, we remember that prayer is the Spirit's work; even if we doze off, the Spirit unites us constantly with God.

When you set aside a special time for prayer, try to use not only your mind, will and emotions when you pray but also your memory, your imagination, your voice in song, your body in gesture or dance. The more that your whole person is engaged, the more of you can be offered and can be transformed by the Spirit into perfect prayer. Please take a moment now to reflect on your past experiences of prayer.

- How would you describe your personal prayer? your family prayer? your parish prayer?
- What was your teenage prayer like? How did it change? What caused the change?
- Move through the decades of your life. What changed your relationship with the Lord? How do you feel about this change?
- What do you hope for in the future in this relationship with the Lord? How much do you want it? How will you pursue a deeper relationship?

The Guided Prayer Passages for reading and praying with Paul's letters, to be found at the end of each chapter, will introduce you to the man and his message according to the themes in this book. These prayer passages are only meant as tastes, and the guiding questions are only examples of how to begin what I hope will be your lifelong prayer pilgrimage with Paul. I recommend only one passage a day. Sometimes I would advise you to return to the same Scripture passage the next day but to pray differently with it. When I use the title "Lord" I mean Jesus, the risen Lord, and thus use masculine pronouns.

Another way of praying with Paul is to read slowly through one or several of his letters. Stop when the Spirit moves you to savor a sentence, to remember a similar experience in your own life, to speak to the risen Lord.

Sharing Faith

Although you may choose to use these prayer passages for personal response to God's word and the Scriptures, it is more consistent with a biblical spirituality to share the word in a group. It may be that a married couple, local religious community, or priests' support group can share their journey through the above Scripture passages. I would encourage each reader to form a small group of 5–8 members who would commit themselves to a weekly meeting to share how God worked through their scriptural prayer.

Each group would need to set certain ground rules for itself about maximum time for a meeting, confidentiality, refreshments, etc. I would insist on just one rule for faith sharing: that no one make any verbal response after each member has spoken. To avoid verbal comment will be a difficult discipline because so many of us want to assure others that we understand and appreciate their journey in prayer. However, even compliments are judgmental, and it is judgments which we must learn to overcome in the faith sharing process.

Sometimes our first judgment is, "Oh, I understand! I had

an experience just like that." No, you did not. Everyone's relationship to God is unique and mysterious. In verbalizing that kind of comparison, you indicate that your mind was rushing back to your own previous experience rather than remaining open to receive the unique experience of the other. Sometimes judgments are comparisons of the other person's depth of prayer or beauty of expression with our own. While occasionally we might judge another's spiritual life as more immature than our own, usually it is *our* religious experience which tends to suffer by comparison. Our minds tell us that each person's journey with and to God is unique, that each person's experience is true. Our culture is competitive and comparing, however, and we need to discipline ourselves to be counter-cultural.

If we can keep from verbalizing our judgments, eventually our private evaluation of others' prayer experiences will cease. We will experience a new openness to the multi-faceted activity of the Spirit in each human heart. Thus, the process of faith sharing itself becomes a kind of contemplation in which we are open to and absorbed by the word of God as it is mediated through the experience of another. We do respond to that word by our posture, with our eyes, smiles, intent attitudes of listening. We do respond non-verbally. In over a decade of leading such faith sharing groups, I have noticed how deeply bonded such groups become even without verbal response and undoubtedly just because of such non-judgmental, open response.

I would suggest that each time the group meets you open with a period of silence, 3–5 minutes. Then, each person speaks of his or her response to one or to a number of the passages from Scripture which he or she prayed during the week; it is helpful to allow 2–3 minutes of silence after each person's contribution. Third, a leader needs to call for the conclusion of the meeting with some prayer or hymn or gesture such as a kiss of peace.

Using the exercises which follow the Guided Prayer Passages might also be a part of the faith sharing group's time together. If they are not prepared beforehand, be sure to allow time for reflection before the group works with the exercises. Some people reflect better with pen and paper. Again, try to keep from judging others; a free flow of ideas without fear of judgment can help people experience the power of the Spirit in the group.

Getting To Know Paul

Before we begin our prayer pilgrimage, I want to set forth some presuppositions about Paul and his work. First, I am convinced that the Paul of whom I will write himself wrote 1 Thessalonians (1 Thes), Galatians (Gal), 1 and 2 Corinthians (1 and 2 Cor) Philippians (Phil), Philemon (Phlm) and Romans (Rom). I will use only those seven letters which are surely Paul's. Definitely not from Paul but from later church leaders come 1 and 2 Timothy, Titus, Hebrews and Ephesians. Still undecided are 2 Thessalonians and Colossians. It might be interesting to note whether some of the things which upset you about Paul and his teaching were really written by him, or by those using his name and authority.

Second, we have two major sources for understanding Paul the person and his teaching: the authentic letters of Paul and Luke's Acts of the Apostles. I agree with all the scholars that Luke's writing is theological rather than historical. Ancient historians were not so interested in facts, verifiable data, details of events as they were interested in the meaning of events. Thus, Luke can tell the story of Paul's conversion in three different ways, or he can tell the story of conflict between Paul and the Church in Jerusalem in a more dramatic yet more peaceful and symbolic way than Paul will. In other words, we can get an appreciation of the early Church's appreciation of Paul by reading Acts, but for a more accurate account of Paul's work and teaching we need to rely on his own letters.

Third, we undoubtedly do not have all the letters Paul wrote to the communities he established. Nor have we the letters they wrote to him asking for guidance in specific problem situations. Paul often seems obscure or one-sided to us because we do have only a one-sided dialogue preserved for us, and that a culturally conditioned one side.

As you begin your prayer pilgrimage with Paul, I will be praying for you and with you, praying that all of us Christians may claim the power which the risen Lord holds out to us, available to us through our baptism. Sometimes Paul calls it "the power of the resurrection" (Phil 3:10). In Greek, the word "power" is *dynamis,* another name for Spirit. I pray that we might experience the Spirit, the prayer of the Spirit, the freedom of the Spirit, the *dynamis* who is Spirit.

For Further Reading

McDonnell, Rea, S.S.N.D., *Prayer Pilgrimage Through Scripture.* New York: Paulist Press, 1984.

Two of the ten chapters present a more in-depth treatment of Paul's communities in Corinth and Galatia, with passages to pray and exercises to share.

Guidelines for Faith Sharing

1. Each group should set rules about the length of the meeting, confidentiality, refreshments, etc.

2. Begin with a period of silence in which the group centers on the presence of the Holy Spirit and prepares to listen to one another.

3. Do not make verbal responses after each person shares. Rather, respond by means of posture, eye contact, smiles, or an attitude of listening. Everyone need not share at every meeting. A simple statement such as "I would like to pass tonight" serves to let the leader know when to conclude the meeting.

4. Spend a few moments in reflection after each person speaks.

5. When concluding, use a hymn, a prayer or a gesture like the sign of peace.

The Mission, Ministry and Passion of Paul

1. The Mission, Ministry and Passion of Paul

- What do you feel when you think of Paul?
- What do you admire about the man?
- What angers you about him?
- What teachings do you appreciate?
- What statements do you wish he had never written?

Reflect privately. Perhaps it will help to jot down your answers. Some people might want to paint their feelings with watercolors. You might share your responses later in your group.

*   *   *

After the resurrection of Jesus and the experience of his outpoured Spirit, the friends and disciples of Jesus began to proclaim the good news that the rejected, despised, crucified one was vindicated by God and now ruled as Lord of the universe. Heady news! Threatening news, not only to high priests and procurators but to devout Jewish men and women who claimed God alone as Lord of the nations. At first the followers of Jesus announced that the risen one was Messiah. That could be laughed off. A crucified Messiah! Then Stephen and his kind began to hint that Jesus was more. Such teaching could disturb the faithful, divide the Jewish community, weaken respect for the torah which cursed anyone who hung on a tree (Dt 21:23).

A young Pharisee named Saul, in utter devotion to the truth revealed in the Jewish Scriptures, enlisted his energy to combat this new sect of Jews. According to the Acts of the Apostles, Saul was commissioned by his elders in Jerusalem to stop the Jesus movement up north in Syria. Not only was Saul learned in the law, but he was zealous with a burning hope that God's word would find a home in his Jewish community. On fire with passionate love for God and his people, Saul hurried toward the city of Damascus.

Mission

In the Acts of the Apostles, Luke offers us three different accounts of what happened on that road to Damascus (9:1–19; 22:4–16; 26:9–18). Paul himself offers three. In Galatians 1:15–17 Paul simply states that he received a direct revelation. In Philippians 3:4–11 Paul explains how God wrested from him everything he once counted so important. Finally, in 1 Corinthians 15:8–9 we learn that this experience of Jesus the risen Lord changed Paul completely and gave him a mission, made him an apostle of Jesus, the Christ.

Is Paul an apostle? How many apostles are there? What is an apostle? Basically an apostle is one who is sent, *apostolos* in Greek. The word "sent" in Latin is *missus,* the root of our word "mission." According to Paul he was sent to preach the Gospel by the risen Lord himself. As Paul will assert, argue, defend again and again in his letters, the Lord himself made Paul an apostle, gave him his mission.

Are there only twelve apostles? According to Luke there are. In writing Acts, Luke thought it important to replace Judas

(1:15–26) so that the number twelve would be complete again. Luke envisioned the twelve apostles like the heads of the twelve tribes of the new Israel, the Church. Even Luke, however, slipped and once named Barnabas and Paul apostles too (Acts 14:14). In the early communities, it does seem that there are many more than twelve apostles. Indeed, in Paul's own understanding it would seem that experiencing Jesus as risen Lord is closely linked to being commissioned as an apostle (1 Cor 15:8; Gal 1:1, 12). If we hold to Luke's understanding of apostleship, you and I are off the hook; we can never be one of the Twelve. But if we affirm Paul's idea of apostleship, then each of us is a possible apostle. What happened to Paul on the road to Damascus can happen to us although perhaps more gradually. We can have direct experience of the risen Christ, we can be weaned away from all that we thought so important and then, freed, we can be sent by Christ to bring good news. We can journey with Paul on pilgrimage, on mission. To experience the risen Lord as alive and active is to be called to be an apostle.

Sometimes this whole process in Paul's life is called conversion. Saul was not converted from one religion to another. Nor was he converted from a life of sin to a life with God, for Saul was devoted to God completely as a Pharisee. Nor was it just a new intellectual conviction that Jesus of Nazareth was truly the Messiah. From his own writings we learned that Saul was converted from achieving his own salvation by keeping the law, to utter trust that the dying and rising of Jesus was his only way of salvation. To be converted means to have a radical change of mind and heart. Saul's beliefs, judgments, values were all radically turned around from his self-sufficient attempt to earn God's favor to an attachment of his whole person to the person of Christ Jesus.

This attachment was nothing he could produce but was God's free gift to him. Paul (his Roman name) found himself "in Christ." The indwelling was mutual. Some fifteen years after his initial experience he could write, "It is no longer I who live but Christ lives in me" (Gal 2:20). Once he wanted to protect the torah from the new sect of the Nazarenes as the early Christians were first called. Now he was embodying Jesus and carrying on Jesus' own mission of bringing good news to the poor (Lk 4:14–21).

An important aspect of Paul's mission was his preaching to the Gentiles. In the early days of the new community, the Gospel was offered only to Jews, but when persecution scattered its first preachers, they moved on to Samaria and north to Syria (Acts 8:1–4) preaching to Jews and Gentiles alike. It seems, however, that the usual procedure for non-Jews (Gentiles) to become members of the young church, sometimes called The Way, was first to join the Jewish religion through circumcision (males) and a vow to keep the Jewish law. Then initiation into the community of Jesus of Nazareth was accomplished through water baptism. When Paul began his missionary journeys, the Acts of the Apostles notes that he usually went first to the Jewish quarter of a city and would preach at a synagogue service that Jesus, raised by God from the dead, was the Messiah. If the Jews rejected that message (and they often did), Paul would turn to the Gentiles in the town and often would find a more open response. But why, Paul wondered, should these Gentile converts to Jesus have to keep Jewish law since God's love was available freely to them in the dying and rising of Jesus? Gentile Christians didn't have to earn God's love. That love was poured out for everyone in Jesus, even while we were sinners, God's enemies (Rom 5:5–11).

This idea of Paul's was a problem to Jewish Christians who saw themselves as a kind of renewal movement in Judaism. Their devotion to worship in the temple, to the law, to works of justice and charity, was increased by their experience of the risen Lord (Acts 2:44–47). They were simply a sect of Judaism, the Nazarenes, just as there were Pharisees, Sadducees and Essenes. For them, obeying the torah might well have been a wholehearted response to God's love made visible in Jesus. But, Paul must have asked himself, was it a necessary response? Did the law unite or divide the followers of Christ? Could the law become a norm with which to measure spiritual progress? If we can measure, can we trust? In his mission to the Gentiles, Paul had to work out these questions, questions to which we will return throughout this book.

Ministry

Mission is service to the world; ministry is service within the community. Once Jews and Gentiles in the various cities that Paul visited had accepted Jesus as their Savior, Paul would nourish the new communities with further teachings, often staying with them as he earned his living making tents. He, it seems, seldom baptized (1 Cor 1:14–16). Nor do we have any record of his presiding at Eucharist (Acts 20:7–12 and 27:35 are obscure). Rather it seems that Paul would study the Jewish Scriptures (an act of worship and thus ministry in Jewish tradition), learning from them even more deeply what the dying and rising of Jesus meant and how this mystery affected the life of the young community. Sometimes in his letters, Paul continued this ministry of interpreting the Jewish Scriptures so as to light up current situations.

Since there is not only proclamation of God's goodness and grace in Christ Jesus in Paul's letters, but also exhortation as to how the community might respond to such abundant love, it would seem that Paul in person would also exhort the new converts. One of the exhortations common in his letters is to remember the poor in Jerusalem, afflicted as they were by famine. Some of his ministry was devoted to collecting alms for them. After he would leave a young community, his ministry to them included prayers of intercession and thanksgiving, and on-going guidance through letters and personally appointed messengers.

Paul sent many messengers back to communities he had founded. Because he wrote such authoritative letters we might forget the dependence this apostle had on his co-workers, both men and women. Barnabas was his chief colleague for many years in the mission field, according to the Acts of the Apostles. Paul's own major reference to Barnabas is a sad one, of bitter disappointment that Barnabas could not maintain freedom in Christ when confronted by Jewish Christians about dietary laws (Gal 2:13). Eventually these two apostles separated, and Silas, according to Acts, traveled then as Paul's colleague.

Particularly in the greetings and conclusions of letters we can see how extensive and dear is the network of Paul's co-ministers. Some co-workers, colleagues in ministry, do need to be highlighted: women played an important role in the communities founded by Paul. A business woman, Lydia, led the household church at Philippi (Acts 16:13–15). A tentmaking friend of Paul's, Priscilla, taught the brilliant young scholar Apollos (Acts 18:1–3; 26); in Romans 16:3–4 she is commended not only as a co-worker but also for having risked her life for Paul. The message of Chloe and her people to Paul is taken very seriously and seems to have provoked Paul's first letter to Corinth (1 Cor 1:11). Phoebe, a deaconness, acted as an overseer or governor at the Church of Cenchreae near Corinth; she is called *prostatis* which is wrongly translated "helper" but means instead a supervisor or governor (Rom 16:1–2). And all women in the Pauline churches must have prayed in public and ministered through prophecy as the Spirit moved them (1 Cor 11:5).

Passion

We believe in the power of the sick and elderly who suffer and pray for the spread of the Gospel. It may be Paul's suffering and prayer on behalf of his communities which affected the life of the young churches more deeply than his teaching and travels. An important aspect of Paul's ministry and mission was his passion, his co-suffering with Christ. He wants *koinonia*, fellowship, union with the sufferings of Christ (Phil 3:10).

On the one hand we say that Christ suffers no more; on the other hand, Paul's disciples teach us that we fill up what is wanting in the suffering of Christ (Col 1:24). In Luke's account, Jesus still suffers when one of the least is persecuted: "Saul, Saul, why are you persecuting me?" (Acts 9:4). Saul must then have known profoundly how "if one suffers, all suffer" (1 Cor 12:26). The body of Christ, his Church, is being built up, is coming to maturity, but also continues to be crucified. "We bear in our bodies the dying of Jesus . . ." (2 Cor 4:10). Sometimes Paul was called on to "crucify flesh with its passions and desires" (Gal 5:24), not to achieve self-control but in service of the mission. He faced physical pain: hunger, cold, whippings, imprisonments, shipwreck. He endured mental pain: his concern for all the churches, his confrontation with Peter, his alienation from Barnabas, his humiliation by the Corinthian community, his separation from his own Jewish community. He knew spiritual pain, especially his conversion from self-righteousness and his continual hunger for God.

Through his suffering Paul came to know God's own consolation. Paul realized too that what he suffered interiorly or exteriorly formed an ever-deepening compassion in him: "Who is weak and I am not weak?" (2 Cor 11:29). Compassion means, literally, to suffer with, bearing other's burdens. Paul understood that his co-suffering with Christ meant compassion with Christ's body, the community. In suffering we can experience *koinonia,* fellowship, communion, with Christ and his church.

Passion has two other common meanings. One is zeal, having a passion for some ideal, some sport, some material object. Paul's zeal for the Gospel seems admirable to most of us. Yet the second meaning of passion as we find it acted out in Paul's life often can distance us from this apostle. Many Christians actively dislike Paul because he is angry, self-pitying, arrogant. Paul has that passion which means strong emotion.

Paul is a passionate man. He was before he met Christ, and after his conversion he let Christ direct his passion toward preaching the Gospel and toward loving forcefully. When Paul loves passionately, he can be tender and cajoling, like a nurse cherishing a baby (1 Thes 2:7). He can also be furious that God's faithful love is scorned, that Jesus' dying-rising love is ignored, that the Spirit's gifts are used for self-aggrandizement and boasting. His anger can be righteous, but because he is a sinner he can feel hurt and angry when his own love and care are forgotten, misunderstood, even mocked. Sometimes his anger leads him to sarcastic, biting remarks not only to or about his enemies but even to his communities. Paul was the first to admit his weakness and sinfulness. He knew he always needed saving.

Our accusation of Paul as proud may not so much stem from Paul's sinfulness as from our own misperception of how rabbis taught in the first century. When a Jewish rabbi gathered a community of disciples not only would he teach them the torah and its interpretation but he would expect his students to imitate not only his words and values but even his mannerisms. Disciples walked, talked, laughed, ate like their rabbi. Greek philosophers trained their disciples in much the same way. Paul says to his young communities: Imitate me. If you want to live the way of Christ, I will be your teacher, so imitate me: my teachings, values, zeal, compassion. That basically though implicitly is what parents ask of their children. Paul was both father and teacher to his new churches. Neither he nor they would have thought Paul arrogant. He had been greatly gifted by the Spirit, and although he often appears weak before the Corinthian community, he experiences that when he is weakest, God's power is strongest (2 Cor 12:9). Usually he is bold, confident, free.

Perhaps it is we who need to revamp our ideas of what sainthood means, what humility is. We have two thousand years of saints' lives, and they are, for the most part, cleaned up by their biographers. Even Luke is guilty of rosy portraits of Peter and Paul in Acts. Paul's letters are not touched up. He writes passionately because he loves passionately and that means with great tenderness and great fury. Paul is authentic in his letters, a man who needs God's saving love constantly because he has learned that he cannot earn holiness, cannot merit grace but is saved through faith. Faith for Paul means clinging to Jesus, another man of great passion and now the risen Lord.

Guided Prayer Passages

Read Galatians 1 and 2:
God set Paul apart from birth to proclaim the Gospel to the Gentiles. Reflect on the Lord's choosing you as his own "from your mother's womb." When, where, how has his choosing you continued throughout your life? Ask him to show you where he has been present throughout your life. Listen to him answer. Tell him how you feel about this choice and this presence.

1 Corinthians 15:3–11:

When Christ "appeared" to these women and men of Paul's day they were called to be apostles, sent to bring the good news of Jesus' victory over sin and death. The risen Lord still "appears" to us and missions us to use all our gifts for proclaiming good news to the world. "Appear" means to have a very real experience of, to know in your gut that Jesus Christ is risen, alive, at work in your life, and that through your life he can reach the world. If that is your experience, thank him for being so real, so alive in your life. If you are not sure how alive he is to you, ask for an encounter as real as Paul's religious experience on the way to Damascus. Ask to know in your whole self that Jesus is not dead and gone but is alive and active in his body, in you.

Philippians 3:1–14:

Paul had much to be emptied out—garbage, as he called it (vv. 8–9). He clung to the law, to his own holiness; he thought he was good. Now he wants only to cling to Jesus, even if that means sharing his sufferings. Sometimes for us that suffering will mean always running forward, never being finished growing, never being able to congratulate ourselves that now we have "arrived" in the spiritual life. Ask Jesus to strip you of your ideas and values of holiness, that your only holiness and freedom may be Jesus himself, that he may live and die in your day-to-day life, and thus that you may continually know the power of his resurrection.

Philippians 3:1–16:

Have you lost anything, do you count anything as garbage because of knowing Christ? Tell Jesus how you feel about it. What goals do you press forward to? Be honest with the Lord—tell him what you *really* want, even if those wants sound insignificant and maybe "unholy." How does Jesus feel about your goals? Ask him. Talk them over with him.

Philippians 3:1–14:

Christ has taken hold of Paul, and so he presses on to take hold of Christ. Ask God for zeal to know Christ, to experience the power of his resurrection—and, if you are up to it, even to share in his sufferings.

Exercises

■ Imagine yourself sent by your parish or congregation to a small tribe of people who have never heard of Jesus. You know their language but you have absolutely no money and only a year to be with them. What will you say? What will you do?

■ Paul quotes "a saying of the Lord's" only a few times. What words of Jesus come to your mind often? Why? Do you ever use any of Jesus' sayings out loud? Why or why not?

■ Imagine that your pastor (and any other ordained leaders) are called away indefinitely. How would the community operate? Be specific and try to list about twenty things your community would need and/or do. If a crisis came up, where would you turn? Would you write to your pastor? Why or why not?

Further Reading

Donovan, Vincent. *Christianity Rediscovered.* Maryknoll, New York: Orbis, 1978.

Keck, Leander E. *Paul and His Letters.* Proclamation Commentaries. Philadelphia, Pennsylvania: Fortress Press, 1979.

Fitzmyer, Joseph A., S.J. "A Life of Paul," *Jerome Biblical Commentary.* Englewood Cliffs, N.J.: Prentice-Hall, 1968, pp. 215–222.

Perkins, Pheme. *Ministering in the Pauline Churches.* New York: Paulist Press, 1982.

While Keck's, Fitzmyer's and Perkins' writings are fine overviews, Father Donovan's work is a possible life-changing book. He tells his story of bringing the "naked gospel" to the Masai tribe in East Africa. His missionary methodology is much like Paul's, but described in modern idiom and powerful narrative.

Tapes

McDonnell, Rea. *Scriptural Sources of Mission and Ministry.* Canfield, Ohio: Alba House, 1983.

Jesus, the Christ

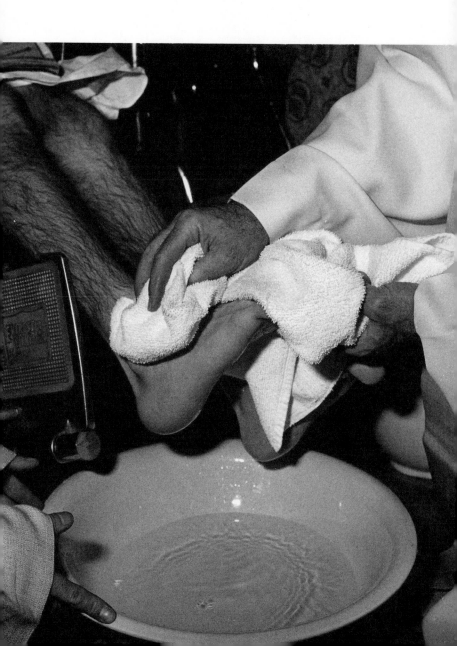

2. Jesus, the Christ

- What is your experience of Jesus? (Knowing, trusting, loving, responding to, etc.)
- How does (did) your family experience Jesus?
- What groups have fostered your experience of Jesus?
- What has been your experience of Jesus in your parish? Where have you discovered him? In people? In liturgy? In other sacraments? In the leaders? In parish events?
- What has been your experience of Jesus in your diocese, country, worldwide church denomination?

You may want to reflect on these questions alone, in your family, or in a specially gathered group of adult Christians.

*   *   *

Jesus is central to Paul's life, thinking, choosing, loving, feeling. All Paul wants to know, he writes, is Christ Jesus. His entire energy, it seems, is spent probing the mystery of Christ, coming ever more deeply, more intimately to know him. For a Hebrew, to know means so much more than apprehending with the intellect. It means to be intimately united with, a verb used in Hebrew even for the act of sexual intercourse. Instead of closing down his mind and heart before the great mystery of Christ, Paul seems to realize that mystery is infinitely know-able. Mystery calls for our continual contemplation and ever more conscious, free surrender. Paul is always engaged with the mystery of Christ.

Faith in the Risen Lord

Paul met the risen Lord on the road to Damascus in a powerful religious experience. Although our experience of Jesus as risen or as Lord probably won't be as dramatic as Paul's, real religious experience is possible for all of us. "Who are you?" we too keep asking the Lord, and year by year the answer varies as we know him and respond to him more completely. Paul never knew Jesus "in the flesh," never met him or talked to him face to face. Yet Paul knew him, as you and I are invited to know Jesus—not to know facts about Jesus but to know him in the Hebrew way, a knowing which is at the same time a loving trust.

This book is a prayer pilgrimage with Paul. Where can Paul lead us in our prayer, which simply means our relationship with God in and through Jesus? How can Paul's knowing, loving, entrusting himself to that mystery who is Christ light up our own relationship with God?

Paul never met Jesus in the flesh. If he had known the historical Jesus, eaten supper with him, talked far into the night with him, worshiped with him in the temple, laughed at his jokes, managed the crowds for him, then Paul in his preaching could return to their shared history, the good old days when he and Jesus traveled together. Instead, Paul wants to know Jesus not by fact, verifiable data, historical memories, but by faith. Faith in Jesus, the risen Lord, means for Paul that he cannot trust any *thing*, any *fact*, any *memory*, but has to trust the religious experience with which God has graced him. God has introduced Paul to the risen Lord and Paul's faith means trusting God's love, God's revelation of who God is in Christ Jesus.

Notice how faith for Paul does not mean "intellectual assent to divinely revealed truths." Faith means knowing a person and surrendering in love and trust to that person. For Paul, faith means clinging to Jesus. Those words may annoy or distance some of us who prefer a more rational, less intimate definition of faith. Yet Karl Rahner, a contemporary Catholic theologian, invites us to have "the courage to throw our arms about him."

Living "in Christ"

The reality is, for us who are baptized, that we are, in all our weakness and sin, already surrendered to the risen Lord. We don't always reflect on that reality. Paul expresses his reflection and resulting action as "pressing forward to take hold of Christ who has already taken hold of me" (Phil 3:12). We are, Paul often writes, "in Christ Jesus." To be in Christ Jesus is not to live in a cosmic, mystical atmosphere but to live, as Barnabas Ahern, C.P. has said, in "an intimate bond of affection and dependence uniting two real persons." Being "in Christ" is like being "in love"—a suffusion of our whole life, not a statement of doctrine or of belonging to the Church.

In fact, the rest of our prayer pilgrimage will simply be a spelling out of what our being, knowing, loving, doing "in Christ" is about. In a sense, this prayer pilgrimage is a reflection on the meaning of our baptism into Christ Jesus. We will first look at how God's love is poured out in Christ while we are not only sinners but even God's enemies (Chapter 3). The dying and rising of Jesus (Chapter 4) is where Paul locates God's love poured out in history. The Spirit of Jesus (Chapter 5) is another expression of God's love poured out in Christ. Being in Christ means being the body of Christ, the visible sign of God's love poured out. Finally, because of God's love for us in Christ, we are gifted with love for those others who are in Christ (Chapter 6).

Wherever we go in our prayer pilgrimage we journey "in Christ" who has taken hold of us as really as he took hold of Paul. Jesus is God's love poured out, the ultimate gift of God's own self. That love of God—that unconditional, abundant, extravagant, faithful, everlasting love of God is made available to us "in Christ."

Guided Prayer Passages

Romans 8:28–39:

Verse 32 can be translated: If God has given us God's own Son, how can God fail to lavish on us all God has to give? We might expect God to give us all we need, but to give us *all* God has to give? We might expect God to mete out all we need, but to *lavish* on us? God wants to lavish. What in me blocks God's lavishing on me? Ask for the grace to receive *all* that God wants to give. In verses 38–39 we learn that NOTHING, not even mortal sin, will make God stop loving us. How do you feel about that? Tell God. Sing! Dance! Cry! Laugh!

2 Corinthians 3:7–18:

If Moses' experience of God was so overwhelming that the people could not look at the radiance of Moses' face, how much more glorious is our experience of God through Jesus and the Spirit. We see God in the face of Jesus. We know God through knowing Jesus. In that knowing we are being transformed more and more into the likeness of the glorious Christ. How much do you want this transformation? How much do you want the freedom which the Spirit offers? The Israelites were suddenly afraid of their freedom and began to long for the "fleshpots" and the security of slavery in Egypt. What are the "fleshpots," the securities in your life? What will being set free mean in your life? Tell the Spirit of your desires but, just as honestly, of your fears. Then rest in the Spirit and ask to trust.

Philippians 2:5–11:
"Have this mind in you which was also in Christ Jesus . . ." Jesus was of a mind to empty himself, even to experience alienation from his Father in the simple fact of being human. He did not cling to being God. To what do you cling? Instead of scraping your conscience, ask Jesus to show you. Of what do you want to be emptied? Try to listen to him tell you. Ask Jesus to bring you into the lifelong process not only of being emptied but of being filled. Ask Jesus to cling to you while you try to cling to him.

Exercises

■ *Baptizo* in Greek means to be immersed in. To be baptized into Christ means to be plunged into him, immersed in him. How did you think of baptism when you were a child? Did the meaning of baptism change for you over the years? Why? How? Some meanings of baptism are: immersion in Christ; forgiveness of sin; inclusion in the body of Christ, the Church community; the source of God's life within us; putting on the mind and heart of Christ . . . and more. Which of the above speaks to your experience? Why?

■ Once Christians were taught to "prove" the resurrection, to "prove" Christ's divinity. But what we can prove we need no longer believe. What has faith meant to you over the years? How has the meaning of faith changed? Do you know any people whom you could describe as faith-filled? How do they act? How do you link beliefs *about* Jesus with belief *in* Jesus?

■ Switch into a faith sharing atmosphere. Take some quiet time to reflect. Share some beliefs *about* Jesus which are precious to you. Conclude with silent or spoken prayer for a deeper belief in, trust of, clinging to the person of Jesus.

For Further Reading

Rahner, Karl, S.J. *The Love of Jesus and the Love of Neighbor.* New York: Crossroad, 1981.
    A difficult, small, and unfortunately expensive book. Rahner summarizes his section on the love of Jesus: "In Jesus, God has come absolutely close to me."

Grace and Sin

3. Grace and Sin

- Instead of constructing a definition of grace, reflect on your personal experience of grace. Remember certain events, persons, desires, insights, choices, etc., that were grace for you. What did these various experiences have in common? What happened to you because of grace?
- What did sin mean to you as a child? As a teenager? What does it mean to you now?
- How did your experience of sin change?
- What are the current situations in which you find yourself limited, weak? How do you feel when you discover a new physical, spiritual, or relational limit?

*　　　*　　　*

Only if we experience grace can we know our sinfulness. This was what happened to Paul on the road to Damascus. As he traveled north, he was satisfied with himself. Not only did he think he was sinless, he thought he was perfect. But when, in a flash, he came to know Jesus, he could, for the first time, see just how sinful and self-serving his very religious life had been. He was, as a zealous Pharisee, busy saving himself. He had no need for God. Salvation was Paul's project, not God's.

Then Christ took hold of him. As Paul was brought more and more deeply into the mystery of Christ he began to see his sinfulness and neediness, and began to count his law-keeping, his spiritual credentials as so much garbage (Phil 3:4–14). When he knew how dearly he was loved by Christ he could let down his defenses, his self-won perfection, and be who he was in Christ: a weak, needy sinner incredibly loved just as he was. He was graced before he could lift a finger to earn grace.

Grace

Many of us are accustomed to think of grace as some thing, a free gift of God, perhaps even God's own life. Grace, however, is not so much a thing as a Person, not so much a static gift as a dynamic process, not so much God's life packaged and given but the very activity of God's giving his own life and love to us. God pours out unconditional, extravagant love and that pouring out, that lavishing is grace. Grace cannot be achieved or merited. God is free. When God wants to lavish love on us, it is freely lavished, not a reward for any work or good deed. God's unconditional love helps us be free too, free to admit who we are, to admit our weaknesses, our rebellions, our self-complacency, our hates and prejudices and manipulations of others. God doesn't ask us to change before he will love us, to shape up. God just keeps pouring love into us, even if we make ourselves God's enemies (Rom 5:5, 10). Nothing can separate us from the love of God. Perhaps not in a flash, but gradually that love frees us, transforms us (2 Cor 3:17–18).

Yet we can refuse to be loved so extravagantly. We can blush and say we're not worth it, we're no good, we're so sinful. We can scrape our consciences and take our spiritual pulse and squelch the movements of the Spirit within us all in the name of growing in perfection. Soul-scraping, however, is not a true acknowledgment of our sinfulness but a self-centeredness which poses as humility. Our eyes are fixed firmly on ourselves instead of on Jesus. We need to be converted from this wallowing in guilt.

On the other hand, a true sense of creaturehood and sinfulness is God's gift to us which can cause us to rejoice in our littleness or boast of our weakness, as Paul put it. When we are weak then God's power is strong to save. Where sin abounds, then the pouring out of God's own self (grace) more abounds. When great saints would confess how sinful they were, they were not pretending. The nearer they were led to God's own holiness, love and fidelity, the more their sinfulness, selfishness and faithlessness were highlighted. They clung to Jesus in all that weakness, not to their own goodness or ideal of perfection, and through Jesus God saved. Some of us, however, like Paul, need to be converted from our goodness, our attempt to create our own justification.

Not only did Paul experience himself personally saved but he knew the world, even sinful Greco-Roman society, to be reconciled to God through Christ. The offer of personal and societal reconciliation was made available in Christ for all those who would accept it. Paul expressed some of the wonder of this reconciliation when he wrote: "In Christ there is no Jew nor Greek, no slave nor free person, no male nor female but all are one in Christ Jesus" (Gal 3:28). The barriers are broken and reconciliation is effected. Social sin has been conquered: racism and nationalism (Jew/Gentile); classism (slave/ free); sexism (male/female). Even the created universe, nature itself, is reconciled and graced (Rom 8:22–23).

That all sounds quite theoretical because we find so much racism, classism, sexism in our society. Creation does groan, as Paul writes, but in our day it groans under the burden of pollution. Even graced as we are, knowing ourselves to be delivered from sin, we find ourselves caught in both personal and societal evil. The way Paul understands this ambiguity in which we live is an "already/not yet" dynamic. The universe is already reconciled, but not yet. We are already dead to sin, and not yet. We have all been raised with Christ, and not yet. It seems that many of us can resonate with that in our own experience. Already/not yet. We are graced sinners.

Sin

The experience of being graced "promotes us to sinners" as Brian McDermott explains in *What Are They Saying About the Grace of Christ?* When we know how loved and saved and grasped and claimed we are, we can dare to be what we are in all truth: loved, graced sinners. That was Paul's experience and may explain some of what we may label his arrogance. He knew without a doubt that he was so special to God, not because he was holy, zealous, loving, but because as sinner he was in Christ Jesus and thus saved.

Paul had various ways to describe sin and its effects. He might term it disobedience, but not disobedience to law or human authority but to God. He might point out our sinful tendencies and unredeemed areas of living and loving which he called "flesh"—*sarx*. He even calls mortal sin our efforts to justify ourselves by keeping God's law. Perhaps in his anger with the Galatians he overstates his case, but he does insist that there is one way to be cut off completely from Christ: You are severed from Christ, you who would be justified by the law; you have fallen away from grace (Gal 5:4).

Why is Paul so adamant about our freedom from the law of God? His insistence seems to flow from his personal experience of being saved and freed from the law, the torah. If we use the law, thinking that we can achieve salvation, holiness, then Christ died in vain, he writes. What meaning did that terrible crucifixion have if we could make sure for ourselves that we are right with God? We live in ambiguity, always having to trust that Jesus' death and resurrection has righted (the meaning of "justification") the relationship, and continues to free us.

In Jesus' obedience all humankind was at last obedient to God. In Jesus' receiving from his Father all that God wanted to lavish on him—God's own self—we all were opened to God's self-giving. In Jesus we are saved, not by keeping the law. In Jesus we are graced, not by doing good deeds. Faith means union with Jesus, and it is by faith that we are justified and that we have peace with God (Rom 5:1). We cannot measure, we cannot claim, we cannot be sure. In the midst of ambiguity about our sin and our freedom, we can only trust and cling and respond as best we can to such an extravagant outpouring of God's love and life in Christ Jesus.

Guided Prayer Passages

Romans 5:1–11:
Ask for the grace of really believing this and rejoicing in it. Because Paul knew he was loved this much—even when he was a sinner—he was fearless in proclaiming this good news.

Romans 5:6–11:
Notice the progression. First Paul writes that we were powerless to do good. True, but God loves to help the weak. More, we were sinners. True, but Jesus came to call sinners. More yet, we were even God's enemies—and God still and completely loved us even and because we were running away from such unconditional love. How does this make you feel? Express those emotions to God and Jesus.

Read Galatians 2:20–3:6:
Paul asks how the Galatians came to receive the Spirit—

through keeping the law or believing the Gospel message? How have you come to receive the Spirit? Why does God love you—because you keep the commandments or because you love and follow Jesus? Ask God what makes you so pleasing, so special.

Galatians 3:19–25:

In God's plan, Paul writes, we as youngsters learned and practiced the Jewish law. It was like a tutor, but Jesus has called us to make adult decisions, to learn from him day by day how to cling to him (for that is what Paul means by "faith"). What is more satisfying to you—a set code which you thought established your security with God or a growing relationship with God's Son which gives you another kind of security? Be honest as you discuss this with the Lord. The law *does* make us secure, and we may have to beg him to help us find all our security in him, not even in the law.

Romans 5:1–11:

What difference can salvation make to us unless we really experience how much we need a savior? Ask Jesus to show you where you are full of darkness, unfreedom, sin. Listen to him a while. Then read the passage from Romans and respond to God who gives you this Savior.

Romans 6:2–11:

Sarx is the Greek word for flesh. When Paul writes of the flesh he does not mean body, which is good, but those parts of us which are not yet redeemed. Ask Jesus to light up those unsaved aspects of your person and to bury them in himself. He wants our weakness and sin; he offers to take it from us and crucify it so that we may have abundance of life now, today. Respond to his saving action. Cling to him.

Romans 5:12—21:

Remember all the sin and evil which people have perpetrated through all time: Cain, Nero, the Borgia Popes, Hitler, Watergate, etc. But Jesus' death offered life to everyone. Pray always to accept this life which so many seem to have refused. "Where sin abounded, grace more abounded" (v. 21). Where in your life has your sinfulness itself finally led to grace? Try to make your memories very specific and look for God's love in each situation. Praise and thank God for gracing you in the midst of sin.

2 Corinthians 5:16—6:2:

Only if we know how much we lack peace and unity in our hearts, our families, our country, can we appreciate what being reconciled means. Ask Jesus to show you where in your own heart or in your relationships you need reconciliation. Then read the passage and respond to him.

Galatians 3:28:

"In Christ there is no Jew nor Gentile, no slave nor free person, no male nor female." Can you remember a time when you felt discriminated against? Was it because you were a woman or a Catholic or a certain nationality or economic class? Remember the incident as vividly as possible, see the people involved, hear them, refeel your emotions at the time. Then stop. Watch Jesus walk into the situation. What does he do, say? To you, to the other(s)? How can you respond to him? Pray to have racism, classism, sexism, nationalism removed from you and from the Church around the world.

2 Corinthians 12:1—10:

The Lord's power is the theme of this section. When have you seen Christ's power at work in your limitations, weakness, frustration, hardships, even in being misunderstood or "persecuted"? After looking at your life with Jesus, narrow it down to just this week's setbacks. Ask him to be strong in your weakness.

2 Corinthians 12:1–10:
Ask the Lord to reveal times in your life when you were weak, but his power was strong in you. Savor the concrete memories of God's care and ask for deeper trust in God's saving power.

Exercises

■ Read Romans 8:19–20. Then take a walk and look deeply at nature, enjoying the beauty and responding. Later watch the TV news and see in what ways we human beings have frustrated nature, shackled it. Try to feel the tension in nature itself—both the beauty and the terror. Bring your observations to your group. Be concrete as you describe the beauty and freedom of your nature walk. Be specific as you describe the distortion of nature which you witnessed on the news. Conclude by reading Romans 8:19–20 aloud and praying together.

■ Singing is twice praying, wrote St. Augustine. The Methodists believe that hymns are excellent educators. Make a group list of twenty or so favorite hymns. Do they celebrate grace or sin? What do you learn about grace, God's self-giving, through their lyrics?

■ Prepare to share with your group novels, movies, plays, art work, popular songs, etc., which have been experiences of grace for you. Which of them have also taught you about God's self-giving or about sin?

■ Like the wheat and the weeds of Matthew 12:24–30, sin and grace exist side by side not only in the world but in us. Take a week to find symbols of this ambiguity in nature (i.e., shadows of clouds across the full moon), in world events, in your own family-community-parish life. If you include incidents from your personal life of wheat-and-weeds ambiguities, be sure you don't say more than you are comfortable with.

For Further Reading

McDermott, Brian, S.J. *What Are They Saying About The Grace of Christ?* Ramsey, N.J.: Paulist Press, 1984.

Monden, Louis. *Sin, Liberty, and Law*. New York: Sheed and Ward, 1965.

Although many works of art, music and literature illustrate grace and sin, and although many theological treatises try to define them, I recommend these two books for their breadth and clarity. McDermott's descriptions of Jesus' embodying God's love are particularly moving.

The Dying and Rising of Jesus

4. The Dying and Rising of Jesus

- What has been your personal devotion to the crucified Jesus over the years? How would you describe it now? What has been the Church's devotion over the centuries? Now?
- That God had raised Jesus from the dead was the central theme of the first Christian preaching. Very exciting and good news to a desperate, despairing Greco-Roman society. Very exciting and good news to a Jewish society which looked for the end time when God's kingdom would break in with resurrection of all the dead. What impact has Jesus' resurrection on today's society? On your parish's life? On your life? If the impact is little or nothing, what can you do to "preach" that Jesus lives?

*   *   *

God's love and life were totally poured out in the dying and rising of Jesus, the source of our salvation, our reconciliation, our freedom. How is it that Paul and his communities could return again and again to that mystery for constant rejoicing, gratitude, wonder, nourishment? Many of us are left unmoved. "That's just history," commented one young

47

woman; "I move with the Spirit now." "It's hard to be so alone," a middle-aged sister complained, "with Jesus dead and gone."

Yet the dying and rising of Jesus is meant to be the central story of our Christian lives, the major movement of our lives in worship. It is the mystery of faith, the core of the Gospels, what we celebrate at Eucharist, the meaning of baptism, the reason we are community, brother and sister to each other.

If Christ is not risen, our faith, our clinging to him, our commitment to him is in vain, Paul wrote. If the crucifixion didn't happen in history, then we can be wafted off into gnostic fantasy and someday we question whether all our religious experience is delusion.

I propose three very partial responses to the lack of interest which, it seems, so many of us first world Christians have in the good news of God's love totally spent in the dying/rising of Jesus: our fear of powerlessness, our denial of death, and our denial of sin.

Fear of Powerlessness

I believe that many of us find the cross of Christ both a stumbling block and foolishness, just as Paul's hearers of the first century did (1 Cor 1:23). Many in the Corinthian community were enchanted by miracles worked by some Christian preachers who followed Paul ("super-apostles," he calls these opponents—2 Cor 11:5), and were unimpressed by Paul who only wanted to preach Christ, and him crucified. In our day too, Christians might prefer to be associated with the powerful, miracle-working Son of God than with the sweaty, tormented man stumbling on the way to crucifixion. Many Christians have deep beliefs in Jesus as God and cannot bear to focus on the human Jesus who was so powerless.

This need to concentrate on Jesus' divinity and supernatural wonder-working powers may stem from fear, even hatred, of weakness in ourselves, but especially in our leaders and most especially in our God. How could the very embodiment of God, Jesus, embrace this powerlessness, emptying himself for death on a cross (Phil 2:8). We hurry to build up our spiritual as well as our social credentials, our store of merit and grace as well as wealth and power and fame. No wonder the frightened yet willing man of Nazareth headed for crucifixion is such a shock. We despise the powerless.

Denial of Death

The Pulitzer Prize was awarded in 1974 to Ernest Becker for *Denial of Death,* a book which exposes our refusal to accept our finite creaturehood and pinpoints our efforts to escape death—and life. We as a society numb ourselves with TV, alcohol, drugs. We delude ourselves by thinking we control outer space and inner space, the human body and psyche. Yet we feel run out of control by computer, by bureaucracy, by a rising suicide rate, by nuclear stockpiling. Instead of the eager expectation of the end of time and space which Paul encouraged in his communities, we dread a self-inflicted destruction of the world, and bury our dread and helplessness in personal and communal depression. "Who can save us from this body of death?"

Paul asks the above question in his letter to the Romans and answers it as we would expect: Jesus Christ. Jesus Christ crucified in weakness, he might add, Jesus the loser, Jesus who understands in his very gut our human temptation to deny any creaturely mortality, our flight from pain both physical and emotional, our hopelessness in the face of unjust political and religious structures. Because in obedience Jesus accepted these terrors, God could transform him in the midst of them. God raised Jesus from fear and helplessness and failure and mortality. We call God's transformation of Jesus' resurrection, and in his resurrection is our hope. Jesus is the first-born of the new creation, the first-born of many brothers and sisters. "Death, where is your victory? Death, where is your sting?" (1 Cor 15:55).

For Paul this dying and rising was such good news. As a Pharisee, he believed that resurrection was the primary sign of God's kingdom breaking into the created universe, into the human heart. Because Jesus was raised from the dead, Paul realized that the eschatological event was begun. "Eschatological" simply means the experience of the end time, the last things: death, judgment, heaven, hell. The end of the world was beginning with this One first born into new life, this risen Christ.

With great urgency, Paul moved on mission to preach the dying/rising Christ: "For he was crucified in weakness but lives by the power of God" (2 Cor 13:4). The end of the world meant hope for first century folk who were oppressed by the economy, slavery and violence as well as by pagan religions ruled by capricious gods and oracles. God had raised Jesus and soon would send him on the clouds of heaven to gather the chosen into God's kingdom (1 Thes 5:1–11). Paul eagerly invited people to be baptized into the dying of Jesus so that the new and risen life of Jesus could become apparent in their mortal flesh (2 Cor 4:10–11) both now and at the end of the world, expected any day. Paul concludes his first letter to the Corinthians with the familiar early Christian cry of longing: "Our Lord, come!"

Denial of Sin

"Death, where is your sting? The sting of death is sin" (1 Cor 15:55–56). Jesus' crucifixion reveals our sin. When God's love has been completely em-bodied in the man on the cross, completely spent for (*huper* in Greek) us, then grace lights up our darkness, uncovers our sin. We are asked to believe that when we were God's enemies, Christ died for (*huper*) us.

We Christians in today's secular society can trivialize sin, sin which has provoked such great love. We tend to dismiss our sinning, our malice and rebellion, our weakness and pettiness, with, "Oh, God won't care." God must care that Jesus poured out his whole life for us. Hanging on that cross, Jesus attracted every evil, every weakness of the human heart and human society, absorbed it all, broke the cycle of evil by refusing to pass it on, killed the power of it in his obedient, forgiving person. Paul knew that the crucified Jesus broke once and for all the power of sin and death in his own death. Paul reminds us of the source of that death, personal and planetary, which we so fear: "The sting of death is sin."

Theologian John Shea points out that sin seems to take root in two different types of human heart. One heart he describes as the rejected heart which wallows in self-pity and unworthiness and guilt; the other he calls the envious heart, always greedy for new and improved ways of pleasing God to win God's approval. The rejected heart refuses to believe it could be so well loved in the midst of, because of its sinfulness:

> Those who are sure they are not loved,
> and lead lives of quiet lovelessness (p. 158).

The envious heart would rather save itself and mask its sinfulness:

> The heart that has prided itself on purity cannot admit to
> any wrongdoing. It would threaten the very foundations
> of its lovability (p. 160).

Jesus on the cross invites both types of sinning heart to find their hope of freedom from death and sin in him:

> To the rejected he became an event of inclusion;
> To the envious he became an event of unmasking.
> To the bereft he became a banquet;
> to the self-righteous a mirror (p. 167).

The cross, revealing so much lavish love and life, also reveals our sin. The resurrection, revealing so much transformation, reveals our victory with Christ over death and sin.

> Do you not know that all of us who have been baptized into Christ Jesus were baptized into his death? We were buried with him by baptism into death so that as Christ was raised from the dead through the glory of the Father we too might walk in newness of life . . . (Rom 6:3–4).

Faith: Participating in the Dying and Rising

What does all the above mean for our prayer, our growing in relationship with God, Jesus, the Spirit? For Paul and for two thousand years of Christian experience, Jesus' dying and rising was and is the central and most extravagantly loving act of God on behalf (*huper*) of humankind; the act most perfectly embodying God's total gift of self to us in Jesus; the act which unleashes the source of all spiritual life into the human heart and into human society, the Spirit.

God's action in Christ Jesus is not for our contemplation alone. Faith, attachment to, commitment to Jesus means participating with Jesus in dying and rising. We are baptized into his death and resurrection—and that implies much more than the gift of personal salvation. The experience of being cruci-fied/enlivened through our union with Christ frees us for discipleship, mission, ministry, orients us on behalf of (*huper*) others. Our contemplation of God's action, our prayer, is meant to open us for actual and ever deepening participation in Jesus' death and resurrection.

The Christian community has tried to express its delight and gratitude and wonder through telling the story of Jesus' death and resurrection: the Gospel; and through celebrating the presence: the Eucharist. The Eucharist, the community's most profound prayer, re-presents the dying and rising of Jesus. In every eucharistic celebration we acclaim the mystery of faith: Christ has died, Christ is risen, Christ will come again.

We are not meant to be mere spectators in the Eucharist, however. Because through baptism we are baptized (plunged) into the dying and rising of Christ, because we no longer live but Christ lives in us, we find the dying and rising continuing in our daily lives. Just as Jesus had to die daily, facing disappointment, physical aches, misunderstanding, fatigue, anger, fear, conflict, temptation, so we die many times a day to selfishness and sin. We rise many times each day too when we experience affection, success, beauty, union, joy—all the various blessings which crowd the day of the one who has eyes to see. By paying attention each day to the dying and rising of Jesus continued in our simple, sometimes humdrum living, we can bring so much to the Eucharist to celebrate and to share in Jesus' own dying and rising.

> We bear in our bodies the dying of Jesus so that the life of Jesus might be apparent in these same bodies (2 Cor 4:10).

Guided Prayer Passages

1 Corinthians 1:22–25, 2:1–5:
Look for a while at a crucifix. Is this foolishness? Is it weakness? How do you feel? Is it difficult to think of Jesus crucified?

Why? Why not? Are you angry? Afraid? Depressed? Grateful? Wondering? (Remember: there are no wrong ways to feel, or no emotions which are holier than others.) Talk over these feelings with Jesus. Read the passage and respond.

2 Corinthians 4:7–11:
How are the things you suffer like Jesus' agony? Can you remember specific times in your past when life and resurrection joy have sprung from those very difficulties? Ask for the power of the resurrection to become apparent in your life today.

Romans 6:2–11:
Sarx, translated flesh, means those parts of us which are not yet redeemed. Ask Jesus to light up those unsaved aspects of your person and to bury them in himself. He wants our weakness and sin. He offers to take it from us and crucify it so that we may have abundance of life—now. Respond to his saving action, not only in words, as you did in the last chapter, but try dancing, singing, running, drawing, writing a poem.

1 Corinthians 15:42–56:
Here is the Christian hope against our society's pervasive "denial of death." Whether we are dead or still living at the "last trumpet" we shall all be transformed. Tell the Spirit in what concrete ways you want to be transformed now so that the resurrection can begin now in you. "Thanks be to God who gives us the victory through our Lord Jesus Christ." Remember areas of sin in your past life that have been healed and change Paul's line to "Thanks be to *you*, God . . ."—composing a litany of gratitude.

Galatians 2:19–21:
Paul says he has been put to death with Christ on the cross. If you have been baptized, so have you. Look at a crucifix. You

began this prayer pilgrimage hoping to grow closer to God and Jesus. How close do you want to be to Jesus? Really? Share your feelings with him.

Galatians 2:19–21:

"It is no longer I who live but Christ lives in me." The powerless one, the always dying-on-behalf-of (*huper*)-others one, the one made-sin-for (*huper*)-us. Discipleship for Paul does not mean carrying our cross alone but union with Jesus, letting Jesus continue his dying and rising in us. Talk with Jesus about discipleship.

Exercises

- Discussion questions:

Can your group remember the five sorrowful mysteries of the rosary? Can the group remember the fourteen stations of the cross? When was the last time anyone heard a sermon on the suffering and death of Jesus? In your family/community/parish, which is the greater celebration: Christmas, Easter or Good Friday? Was it a new idea for some that the Eucharist is a celebration of and participation in the dying and rising of Jesus? If it was not a new idea, can you remember when and where you heard it? Besides fear of powerlessness, denial of death and denial of sin, why does our first world society shy away from the cross? Or does it?

- Each one in the group should ask ten people, Christian or non-Christian, how long they think the world (this planet earth) will survive. What will be the cause of destruction? Does anyone suggest the second coming of Christ to establish God's kingdom? If you propose that idea to them, what is their response? If they reply that they don't know, ask whether their basic response to Christ's return is fear or joy. Share your results in your group.

■ If your group got a special message from God that Christ would return one year from this day, what would each of you personally feel, do? If you would make any group response, what would/could you do? Be sure to allow time for reflection before answering.

■ Conclude the meeting with prayer, making present through memory those family and friends who are now resurrected with Christ. You might light a Christ-candle or other candle in the center of the group as a sign of resurrection. First take five minutes of silence to address each of your own dead by name, remembering them as vividly as possible. Allow time for any who wish to share an incident from the life of one or two of their loved ones. Then let each group member call out the names of his or her dead/risen loved ones and let the group respond, in gratitude for their mortal and immortal life: "Thank you, Lord."

For Further Reading

Becker, Ernest. *The Denial of Death.* New York: The Free Press, 1973.

Brueggemann, Walter. *The Prophetic Imagination.* Philadelphia: Fortress Press, 1978.
    This Scripture professor deals with numbness which afflicted Israelite society in its prosperity, Jesus' society and our own.

Duffy, Regis A., O.F.M. *On Becoming a Catholic.* San Francisco: Harper & Row, Publishers, 1984.
    An explanation of baptism as initiation into the dying/ris-

ing of Christ, with special emphasis on the cross and Pauline theology.

Shea, John. *An Experience Named Spirit*. Chicago: The Thomas More Press, 1983.

Chapter four is particularly helpful on the topic of the cross. Shea's retelling of Gospel stories is graphic and moving.

The Spirit

5. The Spirit

- What has been your personal devotion to the Spirit over the years: as a child? teenager? adult? What has the church's devotion been like? What groups have fostered devotion to the Holy Spirit?
- Remember some concrete times in your life that you know were Spirit-filled. How did you know they were full of the Spirit?
- There is an ancient tradition in the Church, still alive in the Eastern Churches and gradually returning in the West, to call the Holy Spirit "she," the feminine in God. What do you feel about that? What do you think? (Because the community is too easily divided on this as yet, I will not use feminine pronouns for the Spirit. Neither will I use masculine pronouns, however.)

*   *   *

Paul usually pays attention to how God acts, how Jesus operates, how the Spirit functions rather than explaining philosophical definitions of their beings. To distinguish three persons in a triune God will be for later generations of theologians. In fact, Paul identifies the Spirit with the risen Lord in 2 Corinthians 3:17–18. Paul in his urgent mission knows by experience that the risen Lord is present and active in the outpouring of the Spirit. In other words, the Spirit is the way Jesus, risen, communicates with, moves, bonds, loves his community. The Spirit is the risen Lord's way of existing in the world and in human beings.

Paul sees some major functions of the Spirit to be transformation of the world and the human heart; the bonding of God's people with God, Christ and each other; the freeing of people from slavery to sin, law and death; the gifting of Christians with love, peace, joy and all the fruits of the Holy Spirit, as well as with gifts for mission and ministry.

Uniting Us with God

Because Paul is so God-centered, having been turned from the secret self-centeredness of grasping at perfection, Paul experiences the Spirit of the risen Lord as an expression of God's love poured out in the human heart (Rom 5:5). This love poured out is not a once-for-all event but a continual rush of love. The Spirit continually keeps Paul united with Abba, Jesus' familiar name for his Father (Gal 4:6; Rom 8:15). In fact only in these two Pauline passages and once in Mark's Gospel is this intimate, Aramaic form of father used in the New Testament.

Never does Paul take it upon himself to cry "Abba." The name in both instances is "cried," and only cried by the Spirit of Jesus. It is a passionate call to God as "papa" or "daddy." It is the Spirit's cry but not a disembodied cry. It is a prayer from deep within us where the Spirit also intercedes, pleads for us "with sighs too deep for words" (Rom 8:26). It is a constant cry and plea, a "praying always" for which we can take no credit. It is an unutterable desire for union with God which is itself union with God which we have not nor can ever earn.

To be so close to God means to be aware of God's holiness and our sinfulness by contrast. If our bodies are dead in sin, our spirits are alive in the Spirit, Paul teaches from his own experience (Rom 8:9–11). The Spirit is continually transforming the *sarx* of us, the flesh parts of us which are hidden and unredeemed. The Spirit is continually setting us free from sin, death and the Law. "Such is the influence of the Lord who is Spirit" (2 Cor 3:18). Influence literally means a flowing into, a word which characterizes the gentle power, *dynamis*, of our lavishing God. "Where the Spirit of the Lord is, there is freedom" (2 Cor 3:17).

Freeing Us from Sin, Law, Death

Wherever "the Spirit" manifests itself, in whatever culture, whatever age, institutions are threatened; those charged with maintaining the institutions often attempt to wipe out the Spirit-filled because they are so free. The kings of Israel had the prophets persecuted and executed; the Sanhedrin murdered Jesus. But God made Jesus live and his freedom continues in newer, deeper ways. Now wherever the Spirit of Jesus is present, moving, acting, there is freedom. The personal freedom with which Jesus acted has become available in the unleashing of the Spirit into the lives of all Christians through baptism and in the Eucharist (1 Cor 12:13). Baptism and the Eucharist are sources of the Spirit and freedom from sin, law and death.

So many of us were baptized as infants, however, and have not reflected on and claimed all that our freedom in the Spirit can mean. Indeed, in the manner of the boy Saul, the Jew, the young Pharisee, the rabbinic student, most of us too were brought up tightly bound to and by the law of God. Paul writes after his conversion that if he had not known the law perhaps he would not have focused on sin so much of his pre-Christian life. He became more tempted to sin because the law told him certain actions were wrong. He realized only too well how perverse and conflictual that sin/law dynamic was. It almost drove him wild, and how could he escape (Rom 7:7–25)? His cry was one of desperation.

God changed his cry to "Abba," the cry of the Spirit of freedom. Yes, Paul writes, Christians are free to do anything but he will not let anything make free with him; he will not—by the power of the Spirit—be enslaved by anything again (1 Cor 6:12). Freedom in the Spirit does not lead to license but to a new, non-legalistic way of relating with God. For example, if our bodies are temples of the Spirit then we can hardly abuse them with excesses of food, drink, sex (1 Cor 6:14–20). Instead of avoiding such sin because the law commands or even because of the natural outcome of excess, we reverence our body as the home of the Spirit who continually cries "Abba" from deep within. Instead of a fearful focus on sin, we can enjoy a peaceful focus on the Spirit in action.

Then why is it so hard? It may be that we haven't experienced the Spirit's freeing power in our lives because we never have made a personal choice, an adult decision to claim that power of our baptism, a conscious choice to be buried to sin in Christ Jesus and to be made alive to God. It may be that we are afraid of freedom, that we need to measure ourselves by law to be certain that we are O.K. with God. It may be that we haven't matured to a point where we can even want God's freedom over the warnings of our parents (even if they are long dead) and the conventions of society. Who can save us from this kind of death? The Spirit has already begun! "The law of the Spirit is life" (Rom 8:2).

Gifting Us for Others

Christian life is a life for (*huper*) others. The Spirit gifts us with union and freedom not so that we will feel good or superior but for the sake of others. Paul could write, in his overstating, passionate way, that if only the Jews could accept Christ, he would be willing to be cut off from Christ forever (Rom 9:3). What he means was that he would lay down his life—the only life that really counted for him, life in Christ—on behalf (*huper*) of his brothers and sisters. Greater love . . .

Love and joy and power are often associated with the Spirit in Paul's writings. The outcome of the Spirit's lavishing is a loving life, an attractive witness of joy, a radiant power even when seemingly we are weak. There is a law, Paul writes, which does not enslave us but serves to open us to others. "Bear one another's burdens and so you will fulfill the law of Christ" (Gal 6:2). Where do we get the energy to bear burdens?

The word energy in Greek is *dynamis*, power, a term Paul associates with the Holy Spirit. Just as the Spirit bonds us with God, so the Spirit is that creative energy which unites us with each other. The energy expresses itself in fruits of the Spirit, given to us for the sake of (*huper*) others. Paul calls us to walk in the Spirit, to be led by the Spirit, and then the fruits of the Spirit's activity deep within us will gradually become apparent in our life for others.

How do we know if our life is for others, if our decisions are of the Spirit? If we cannot rely on Jewish law to guide our decisions and actions, then where can we put our trust? Paul answers: in the Spirit who is fruitful. Are we moving toward death or life? Toward slavery or freedom? Toward self-centeredness or other-centeredness? We know we are living in the Spirit if our decisions lead us to gradual growth toward life, freedom, others. We know we are living in the Spirit if our decisions lead us to gradual growth in "love, joy, peace, patience, kindness, goodness, faithfulness, gentleness and self-control" (Gal 5:22–23), the fruits of the Holy Spirit.

All of these gifts of the Spirit are given to us not just for our life and freedom but for the sake of (*huper*) others. Those others are intimately and forever joined with us by the bonds of the Spirit in what Paul has called the body of Christ. These fruits of the Spirit are available to everyone in Christ. Whether union, freedom, energy or fruits, all these gifts of the Spirit are given us for the building up of the body of Christ.

Guided Prayer Passages

Romans 8:14–25:
The Spirit prays constantly within us, even when we are not conscious of the Spirit's action. Mentally move through your day and thank the Spirit for praying within you while you brush your teeth, drive to work, read your mail, tune the TV, correct your children, even sleep. "It is all God's work, nothing which we can achieve" (Ephesians).

Romans 8:26–39:
Because it is the Spirit praying, we will never have a "bad" prayer period. Our feelings may not be all juiced up but all things work together for those who love God. Ask the Spirit to open you up to the realization that you are lovable, lavished upon by the Father.

Romans 8:15:
Spend ten minutes or so letting the Spirit cry "Abba." See if you can hear the Spirit, the cry deep within you.

Philippians 1:4–6, 1:8–11:
What do you long for? For whom do you long? Beg the Spirit to bring what the Spirit has begun in you and through you to completion. As the Spirit overshadowed Mary and made her fruitful, ask the Spirit to form Jesus in your body, your mind and your will.

2 Corinthians 3:12–18, return to vv. 17–18:
As you have worked through this book, how has the Spirit influenced you through your study of Scripture and your efforts at prayer? How has the Spirit transformed you? How do you feel? Tell the Spirit what more you want. Be bold in your desires.

Galatians 5:1
"For freedom Christ has set you free. Let no one make you a slave again." In the past, who or what has enslaved you? How were you set free? How does the memory make you feel? Tell the Lord about your memories and feelings. Ask *him* (not yourself) where he still wants to free you. Ask for the gift of his Spirit.

Romans 6:12–23:
Remember in concrete detail a time when you were a slave to someone or something. Discuss how you felt with Jesus. Ask him to show you what things still hold you captive. Ask him for freedom. Ask him to teach you what obedience to the Spirit (not to the law) will mean.

Romans 8:18–27:
We are in tension between the beauty of our freedom and the terror that arises from being free and responsible. We are groaning and waiting for full freedom. What are your particular tensions? Discuss them with Jesus. Ask for a deeper awareness of and a fuller participation in the groaning of the Spirit.

Romans 8:26:
When has the Spirit come to the aid of your weakness? Be concrete. Imagine those situations vividly. Feel the Spirit present and working in them.

Galatians 5:22–23:

Use Galatians 5:22–23 as a criterion to judge your actions and to make your decisions. Do the decisions you make help you grow in peace, joy, love, kindness, etc.? Remember a major decision you made this past year. Ask the Lord to show you how the fruits of the Spirit have deepened the "rightness" of this decision.

Galatians 5:22–23:

After some activity today, stop and read Galatians 5:22–23. What fruits of the Spirit were present in that activity? How do you feel about that? After some decision you make today, stop and read Galatians 5:22–23. What fruits did you experience after making that decision? How will you respond to the Spirit?

Exercises

■ The Spirit is imaged in Scripture as a breath, wind, fire, dove. How would you, could you, image the Spirit? Draw your image of the Spirit. Does any musical instrument image the Spirit of you? Bring a piece of music to the group and share this type of Spirit-image. Could you act out the Spirit in some kind of bodily movement? Remember that everyone's image, music, movement is correct, and the variety of images only enriches the group.

■ The Hindus call God by a thousand names. The psalmists certainly had many names for God. The Spirit and Jesus call God "Abba." In your group, slowly and unafraid of silences, call out names for the Holy Spirit. Lighting a candle and opening with a prayer asking the Spirit to teach you might set the mood. You can surely use such biblical names as Paraclete, Spirit of Truth, etc. Be creative as well. Range as far as your own experience of the Spirit lets you.

For Further Reading

Farrell, Rev. Edward J. *Surprised by the Spirit*. Denville, New Jersey: Dimension Books, 1973
A practical help for life in the Spirit.

Montague, George T., S.M. *The Holy Spirit: Growth of a Biblical Tradition*. New York: Paulist Press, 1976.
A commentary on the principal texts of the Old and New Testaments which is a bit technical, but very thorough. Father Montague's other writings on the Spirit are always pastoral.

Rayan, Samuel. *The Holy Spirit: Heart of the Gospel and Christian Hope*. Maryknoll, New York: Orbis Books, 1978.
An excellent teacher, Father Rayan brings the experience of his native India to the topic.

Shea, John. *An Experience Named Spirit*. Chicago: Thomas More Press, 1983.
Delightful and deep!

The Body of Christ:
Gift and Gifted

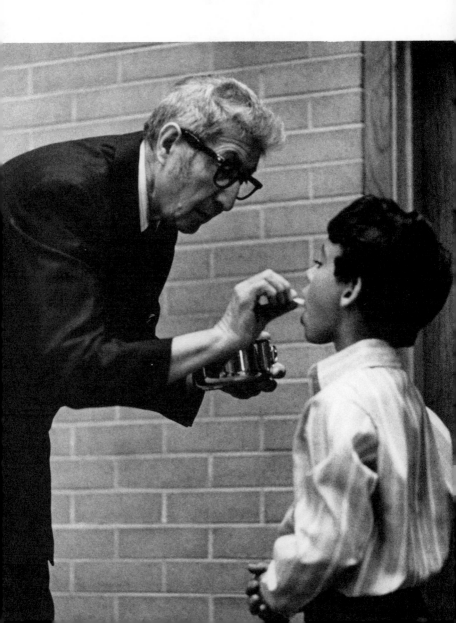

6. The Body of Christ: Gift and Gifted

- Paul describes his experience of the risen Lord in terms of the "body of Christ." That phrase, in turn, colors all his further experience. Each of us probably has an initial, powerful realization of who God/Jesus/Spirit is and what that means. When I was twenty-one I saw an Easter banner which proclaimed: "Jesus lives." We can spend a lifetime letting the depth of that experience unfold for us. What conversion point or insight or decision or relationship has had and continues to have that kind of impact on your life?
- What does the body of Christ mean to you? Has the meaning changed? Can you pinpoint what caused the change in meaning?
- What gifts do people you know have that build up their families, neighborhoods, parishes? What gifts do you have?

*   *   *

Paul's initial experience of the risen Lord was a powerful and lifelong invitation. The risen Lord invited Paul to understand Jesus as extended in space and time, to understand Jesus

73

living through the lives of those who believed in him. "Why do you persecute *me?*" the risen Lord asked, years after the cross/resurrection. "Who are you?" Paul asked in return. According to the Acts of the Apostles, the Lord responded, "I am Jesus of Nazareth whom you are persecuting." This identification of Jesus with the persecuted is similar to Matthew's portrayal of the last judgment: "When I was hungry, homeless, naked . . . whatever you did to the least you did to me." Paul was introduced to Jesus identified with his brothers and sisters, introduced to the body of Christ on the road to Damascus.

Some scholars hold that the body of Christ is the most central concept in all Paul's writings. The word "body" in Greek is *soma.*

> . . . the word . . . (*soma*) knits together all his great themes. It is from the body of sin and death that we are delivered; it is through the body of Christ on the cross that we are saved; it is into His body the Church that we are incorporated; it is by His body in the Eucharist that this Community is sustained; it is in our body that its new life has to be manifested; it is to a resurrection of this body to the likeness of His glorious body that we are destined (John A. T. Robinson, *The Body*, p. 9).

In this chapter we will not concentrate on our own body of sin and death, saved through the crucified body. We will instead focus on the gift of our own bodies-in-process-of-transformation, the gift of Eucharist, and the gift of community, the Church. We pay attention to the body of Christ, now risen, yet the very corporal, tangible way that Jesus' life and whole human person (*soma*) is extended. The body of Christ is not a mystical body if mystical connotes intangible, unreal, merely a metaphor. Rather, the body of Christ is a mystery which we shall never finish trying to understand and experience. For Paul, the body of Christ is no figure of speech, no mere image of reality, but reality itself—quite indescribable, but a reality. Indeed, there may be nothing more real for Paul than that he and we are "in Christ," not in some mythical, mystical cosmic atmosphere but in the very body of Christ.

Gift

To be in Christ is never a solitary experience but always a being with and for others. "In Christ" is a way of saying that the desperate loneliness of modern humanity is assuaged. What the world needs now is interdependence, especially in the face of such massive pseudo-independence of individuals and nations. That interdependence is accomplished "in Christ." Paul, in his exuberance to describe our interdependence with Christ and with each other, seems to coin new words. He writes of followers-together, yoke-fellows, fellow-soldiers. He uses "co-workers" in six of his seven authentic letters, a term not used elsewhere in the New Testament except once in Colossians and once in 3 John. His verbs, used nowhere else in the New Testament, sometimes describe our union with Christ, sometimes with one another: share with, continue with, suffer with, sent with, planted together, have the same mind as, strive together, help together, labor together, groan together, glorified together; and finally, "be made into the same form with" Jesus' death, his glorious body and his image. Paul seems to know that God has myriad ways of uniting us with Christ and with each other.

It is in the body of Christ that we, the baptized, "live and move and have our being." We "put on" Christ's body, baptized into union with him, ". . . for you are all one person in Christ Jesus" (Gal 3:26–28). Many now represent the one. We represent Christ. We are the body of Christ. In the Jewish Scriptures one represented the many, such as the Servant of Isaiah or the Son of Man in Daniel; these two figures stand for the whole of Israel. In Christ, we "who are many are one body for we all share in the one loaf" (1 Cor 10:17).

The body of Christ who we are is (1) the risen body extended in space and time through us, (2) the body which we share in the breaking of the bread, (3) the body-community which we discern in the eucharistic Communion, and (4) the body gifted with many parts and functions. There is no body of Christ in space and time without us, no Eucharist without the offering of the body who is us, no Church which is not us. Christ is not far away sitting on some starry throne; Christ is not a lonely prisoner in the tabernacle. Christ is us, his body, his whole self extended in time and space to this time, to our space so that we can communicate him to everyone we meet.

Because we are the body of Christ, all sin then is against the body. Paul gives us a few examples. To sin against a weaker brother or sister is to sin directly against Christ (1 Cor 8:12). To join our bodies to the bodies of prostitutes is to take the very "limbs and organs of Christ . . . and make them over to a harlot" (1 Cor 6:15). To eat and drink at the Eucharist without discerning the body who is the poor member of the community is to eat and drink not Christ at all but judgment on our lack of love (1 Cor 11:27–32). In other words, if we do not see the body of Christ in every member of the community and especially in the poorer or weaker members, yet we go on receiving bread and wine as though it were *the* body of Christ, we "eat and drink unworthily and are guilty of the body and blood of the Lord" (1 Cor 11:27). Paul uses very strong language, perhaps strange to us who have often privatized the Eucharist, focusing on Holy Communion and our personal bond with Jesus. For Paul, the real presence of Christ is in the community who eats and drinks and remembers. It is in eating the one bread that Christians become one body, the body of Christ (1 Cor 10:16). To remain in isolation, to shut out one or many of the body, even if we eat and eat and eat, will produce nothing more than judgment.

Grace too is located in the body. We have died to law through the body of Christ and are joined to the one raised (Rom 7:4). Through his body we have access to God. Grace is located in the body which is the Church. We the Church belong to each other. God makes the ultimate self-gift (grace) through the body of Christ, the risen Lord, living and acting in his members. Note that we are not one body in Christ, not a moral or social entity gathered together in Christ. We are the body *of* Christ (1 Cor 12:27). We are incorporate in him. The root of that verb is *corpus,* Latin for body. The resurrection of Jesus has transformed, expanded his human limits and he is able to welcome us all into himself, to make us his body. It is the resurrection which makes a real, not metaphorical, identification between Christ and the Church. Later New Testament authors will separate the community from Christ, naming Christ the head of the body, naming the Church the bride of Christ. Not so in Paul's experience. The Church *is* the body of Christ.

Grace is located in our own human, sinful, yet in-the-process-of-being-transformed bodies. It is into our bodies that the Spirit is poured, crying "Abba." We do not belong to ourselves: ". . . the body is for the Lord . . . for you were bought at a great price. Glorify God therefore in your body." Our bodies are God's gift, temples of the Spirit (1 Cor 6:13–20). Our bodies are sources of grace for each other (1 Cor 7:14).

Gifted

Sex, Marriage, and Celibacy

Our bodies are sources of grace for each other. Perhaps in no other area of Christian living has Paul been so misinterpreted as in the area of sex and marriage, and, by extension, in his supposed treatment of women. Paul's teaching needs to be examined directly from the Scriptures, preferably using two or three different translations for comparison. The Revised Standard Version is the most literal, closest to the the the original Greek.

I treat sex and marriage under the topic of "gifted body" to try to counteract the still prevalent belief, at least in Roman Catholic circles, that celibacy is the best way of discipleship, with marriage a safety net for those without self-control. What does Paul say? The first letter to the Corinthians, chapter 7, offers the most reflection on the two different life-styles: celibacy and marriage, both gifts of God for the building up of the body which is the Church. These are *the* two vocations, two different life-styles. All other ministry, be it politics or priesthood, medicine or mothering, praying for or playing with the disadvantaged, is done from our basic commitment in marriage or in celibacy. Thus there is nothing in Paul's teaching on marriage/celibacy which rules out marriage for a modern priest. There is nothing in Paul either which cancels the gifts given for priestly service, should those gifts exist (and they do!) in the married, be they men or women.

Please open your Bible to 1 Corinthians 7 and follow along with me. Paul is responding to questions raised by his young community located in the "sin city" of the ancient world. Orgies and promiscuity were rampant. Many of the new Christians had just recently left that life of debauchery. In their fervor, some of them went to the other extreme and decided to abstain from sex even in marriage. "You say, it is good for a man to have nothing to do with women . . ." is not Paul's teaching; he is quoting their misguided thinking.

"The husband must give the wife her due" is a startling statement in favor of women. In Jewish society a woman had absolutely no rights; in Greek society she was scarcely more honored. Being "in Christ" changes the relationship in marriage and makes the partners equal: "In Christ there is no . . . male or female for you are all one in Christ Jesus" (Gal 3:28). Even more startling is Paul's teaching on mutuality in marriage: "The husband cannot claim his body as his own; it is his wife's."

Verses 6–8 have always been interpreted that Paul himself is celibate, or at least widowed. There is no basis in the Greek text for the word "single" which English translations often insert. Indeed later in the letter (9:5), Paul asks why he is criticized for bringing his wife/woman (the word *gyne* means both in Greek) when the other apostles and Peter bring their wives. Suppose that "stay as I am" (7:8) means devoted totally to evangelization as Paul was. Whatever focuses the desire of the married, the unmarried and the widowed on the work of the Lord is the "gift God has granted" (7:7), whether in marriage or celibacy.

At a time when the major Jewish rabbis permitted a man to divorce his wife for putting too much salt in his food, the saying of the Lord against divorce must have offered Jewish-Christian women refuge from arbitrary divorce. Paul implies that in her new freedom "in Christ," a Christian woman as an equal to her husband could divorce her husband (never in Judaism), but she should not.

Verses 14–16, so often interpreted for their legal ramifications, is one of the most beautiful expressions of what a Christian family is. A Christian spouse is a channel of grace for the non-Christian spouse. A woman's body, a man's body, their sexual union, their daily living in love are sources of grace, of union with God. Their love, in all its aspects, is sacrament. Because of one Christian parent, a whole family is consecrated to God. The early Church did not baptize infants because, according to this teaching, belonging to a Christian family, with even one Christian parent, joined the children to

God. Spouses did not have to work at converting their non-Christian partners. They could rejoice in the sacramentality of their own bodies and lives. "Think of it!" Paul exclaims, hymning both marriage and, in such a radically different way for a former Jewish rabbi, women: "Wife, you may be the means of your husband's salvation!"

A digression here about a supposed word of Paul to women which he really did not write. In 1 Timothy 2:15, the author of the three pastoral letters (1 and 2 Timothy and Titus) tells women: "By your childbearing you will save your souls." Exalted as the Christian family may be for Paul, nothing saves us but the dying/rising of Jesus. We do not save our own souls no matter how worthy the work. Also, as we shall see as we continue our study of 1 Corinthians 7, Paul did prefer that women remain celibate if they were so gifted so that they could devote themselves to the ministry.

The next section of 1 Corinthians 7 presents Paul's puzzling passivity in the face of slavery (vv. 17–24) but provides a context for what follows on the topic of celibacy. Paul was utterly convinced that with the resurrection of Jesus, the end time had begun, that God was gathering the nations (same word as Gentiles) together as Isaiah had promised, and that the time was short before the return of the risen Lord in glory, the parousia. Paul eagerly joined God's work as an ambassador of reconciliation (2 Cor 5:19–20), especially oriented to the pagans, the Gentiles. He was urgent in his preaching the good news and he hoped to enlist as many of the newly baptized in his urgent mission. "This world as we know it is passing away" (7:31). How to focus our energy in such apocalyptic times? Paul offers a way to focus in verses 32–35, a variation on Jesus' own saying that celibacy is a gift but only for the sake of the kingdom, not because it has any value in itself (Mt 19:12). We can easily imagine male celibates engaged in preaching and teaching, exhorting: "Be reconciled, for the time is short." What is remarkable about Paul is that women "co-labored" with him, probably some at his express invitation, probably some celibate women like Phoebe of Cenchreae, an officer "on mission" to Rome (Rom 16:1–2).

Verses 36–38 are obscure in the ancient manuscripts, perhaps because the custom had become obscure to the copyists of the manuscripts. I prefer the New English Bible's: "If a man has a partner in celibacy . . ." It seems unusual in the Greco-Roman society still repressive to women, at least lower class women as many Christians were, that a woman celibate could manage on her own without scandal. There is the possibility of a non-genital man/woman relationship in which both partners would be devoted to the Christian mission. If their love becomes genitally oriented "there is nothing wrong in it; let them marry. . . . Thus, he who marries his partner does well, and he who does not will do better." Does that last clause destroy my whole argument about separate but equal gifts of marriage and celibacy? Perhaps, but Paul is not against sex, marriage or women. He simply urges the Corinthians, because the world will end any day, to devote their entire selves to the mission. That kind of freedom comes more easily for the unmarried.

In reinterpreting Paul on marriage I would not want to downplay the gift of celibacy which I believe will be given always to certain members of the body for the sake of the kingdom. Religious congregations of women and men where celibacy has found a structure to protect and nourish it may disappear, but the gift will flourish. Sexual abstinence which poses as religious celibacy will have to be purified of psychological fears and/or sociological power, but the gift for the sake of mission will flourish. Celibacy can lead to human intimacy and permanent commitment; marriage can lead to freedom for ministry. Neither way is higher or more perfect. Both are for the building up of the body.

Charisms for Ministry

Union with God and with each other, freedom and its energy, and the fruits of the Spirit are available to all Christians. Some members of the body, however, have special gifts for special services (the Greek word is *diakonia*, also meaning ministry). Twice Paul lists some of these gifts for ministry given by the Spirit for the sake of the community, the body of Christ. Romans 12:4–9 is a summary of his more detailed description of Christ's body and the functions of its members which is found in 1 Corinthians 12—13. Sometimes, as with marriage and celibacy, Paul mentions gifts apart from these two lists. Sometimes, different generations in the Church's history have named other gifts for ministry. These gifts can be called by their Greek name: charisms.

In the Corinthian community the gifts of the Holy Spirit were abundant. Paul, however, has to devote quite a bit of his first letter to them addressing their particular situation in which manifestation of the gifts could become disruptive of the community and a scandal to those interested in joining. In 1 Corinthians 11:2–12, Paul explains how men and women should dress when they use their gifts of public prayer and prophecy. (Note that in this passage, Paul begins by using the Jewish hierarchy of authority: God/Christ/man/woman. He concludes, however, by correcting himself: "In the Lord, neither woman without man, nor man without woman . . . but all are of God" [v. 12]; in Christ, there is new equality of women and men.)

Then after discussing the body at the Eucharist, Paul moves on to explain the body with its various parts, functions and gifts. The first of the spiritual gifts is the Spirit's own self, manifested in the heart-cry: Jesus is Lord!

> There are differences of gifts (*charismata*)
>   but the same Spirit.
> There are differences of ministries (*diakonia*)
>   but the same Lord.
> There are differences of workings (*energemata*)
>   but the same God,
>   the One working all things in all (1 Cor 12:4–6).

A variety of gifts are then listed, all manifestations of "the same Spirit." The Spirit is the source both of the body's unity and of its diversity.

Later on in chapter 12, Paul lists specific functions of various members of the body, placed by God in their roles of apostle, prophet, teacher, wonder worker, healer, helper, governor, speaker in tongues. These roles/functions/gifts are to operate as interdependently as do the various members of the human body: feet, ears, eyes, etc. (12:14–24). The point is, Paul insists, that there is not to be division (*schisma*) in the body but the members should "care for one another. If one member suffers, all suffer together; if one member is glorified, all rejoice together" (1 Cor 12:25–26). To suffer with is the literal meaning of com-passion; to rejoice with is the expression of Christian love.

"The Greatest of These Is Love"

We have been thinking hard and need a pause. Stop and reflect:

- What is your experience of being loved? Earliest memory? Dearest friend? Various friends/children loving you in various ways? Greatest sacrifice for your sake? Quietest, shyest action of love offered you? Most recent experience? Who, when, where, what, how, why?
- What is your experience of loving? Earliest memory? (Etc.,

using same questions as above.) Hopefully, you are in a quiet, happy feeling state. "Rest a while."

At the end of his list of gifts in Romans 12:4–8, Paul has a hymn to love, much less known than the one of 1 Corinthians 13 which concludes the list of charisms in 1 Corinthians 12. We are familiar with the Corinthian hymn: "Love is patient and kind . . . not arrogant or rude . . . faith, hope, and love remain, but the greatest of these is love." In Romans 12:9–13, Paul marshals participles in the Greek:

> Let love be genuine: shrinking from evil, clinging to good, loving warmly, preferring one another, in zeal not slothful, burning in spirit, serving the Lord, rejoicing in hope, enduring in affliction, steadfastly continuing in prayer, sharing the needs of the saints, practicing hospitality.

The hymn continues to elaborate on sharing (*koinonountes*) with the saints which Paul calls all Christians: "Rejoice with those rejoicing, weep with those weeping" (12:15).

There is for Paul a kind of ultimate consequence of being together in Christ: compassion. Rejoicing with, weeping with, suffering with (1 Cor 12:26), being with, thinking with (Rom 12:16) feeling with one another. Paul leads the way in getting inside the other. "I am as you are," he writes the Galatian community. "Be as I am because I am as you are" (Gal 4:12). "Who is weak and I am not weak?" (2 Cor 11:29).

He can only lead the way, however, because he has first experienced God as the Father of compassion and the God of all comfort (2 Cor 1:3; Rom 12:1). If God wants to get inside us, pouring God's own self into our hearts (Rom 5:5), then Paul understands the Gospel command of love not as command but as *koinonia*, sharing, participating in God's own compassion. If we must have law, then "bear one another's burdens and so you will make full the law of Christ" (Gal 6:2).

In Romans 13:8–10, in the context of justice in the public sphere, Paul does use a kind of legal language: "Owe no one anything except to love one another." He explains how Jewish commandments are summed up in the law of love. Yet Paul does not offer an ethical code, a moral system. Love is a spiritual gift, a charism, one of the fruits of the Holy Spirit, a share in God's own love made available in Christ Jesus. The bond of the body, the life-blood of the body, the Spirit of whom we all drink (1 Cor 12:13), the greatest of all gifts, is love.

Guided Prayer Passages

I would suggest that when you take a period for prayer you begin by asking the Spirit to pray within you (for the Spirit's prayer is perfect praise) and to show you all God's gifts to you throughout your life. Ask the Spirit to convince you that you are special in the eyes of God, that your gifts are unique, and are needed for the building up of the whole Church-community.

Read Galatians 1 and 2:
What gifts has the risen Lord given you? Ask him—don't try to think and introspect; let it "come" to you as you try to listen to his answer. What is his purpose in gifting you? Ask him. Listen. Tell him how you feel about his gifts to you.

1 Corinthians 12:1–31:
Ask the Lord to reveal what gifts you have (not necessarily those from Paul's list) that are given to you for the building up of the body (your family, your community, your country).

1 Corinthians 12:4–11:
Think of someone you know who has a particular gift mentioned. How do you feel about that person? Tell the Spirit how

proud you are of that person, or how jealous. Keep asking the Spirit (every day) to show you what your gifts are. (Probably many not mentioned here; if you have wrung this chapter dry, you might take any Gospel scene and look at Jesus and his people in terms of gifts, i.e., Zacchaeus. What gifts did Zacchaeus have? What gifts were operating in Jesus? Did Jesus know his gifts? Did he use them?)

1 Corinthians 12:14–26:
Matthew 10:40–41 has much the same message as Paul here. We can't do all the good we would like to do in our lifetime— but our brothers and sisters all over the world are doing a variety of good works, building up the body. If we "welcome" them (accept, understand, appreciate their gifts and their ministry) we receive their reward.

1 Corinthians 6:12–20:
Our bodies are gifts, bought at a great price. Paul speaks about food and sex here. What other aspects of your body concern you? Show your body, part by part, to God who knows every cell of you. Ask Jesus to lay his hands on your head, your shoulders, etc. Let him move slowly down your body. Feel, in your imagination, Jesus claiming each part of your body. Invite him to be Lord of your body as a whole and in every part. Give him your fears about your body, past sins against your body (including neglect), your bodily limits. Give him your bodily strengths, your joy in your body. Give him your whole self.

Romans 12:1–2:
Paul exhorts us to present our bodies "through the compassions of God." Can you believe that God "suffers with," "feels with" you? What feelings arise in response? God becomes flesh, incarnate, in Jesus so that God can share all the weak-

ness, insecurity, pain, weariness of our bodies. God desires the whole of us, our bodies. What response can you make now to God's desire? What response do you hope to make?

Philippians 2:1—8:

Another Pauline hymn of love makes compassion central. "If there is any comfort in Christ, any consolation of love, any community (*koinonia*) of spirit, and gut-level compassion . . ." is a literal translation of verse 1. Ask to know the comfort of Christ; then wait, silent, open to receive. With whom do you have "community of spirit"? With whom do you want it? Family? Co-workers? Neighbors? The homeless and hungry? Folks of another race? Share all this with Christ, present in you and in them.

2 Corinthians 1:3—7:

Ask Jesus to help you remember difficult situations in the past month. Did your living through those difficulties in any way lead you to grow in compassion for others? Ask to have the heart of Christ so you may comfort others in their sufferings. Pray for some of those suffering now.

Galatians 5:13—6:2:

What is the law of Christ? How do we fulfill it? (See verses 18 and 25.) Ask for the fullness of the Spirit who is love and burden-bearer. The Spirit is your power and energy (*dynamis*) to love. Share some of your burdens in loving with the Spirit.

Exercises

■ Anointing is a sign of consecration. In Greek the word for anoint is *christos*. Thus Jesus is the Anointed One, Christ. We were anointed in baptism and confirmation. In memory of that Christ-ening, anoint one another in your group. Use sweet-smelling oil, or add a drop of perfume and sign the cross on each other's forehead, eyes, ears, mouths, hands. "Your body is for the Lord . . . glorify God in your body."

■ Take the hymn to love from Romans 12:9–13 quoted in this chapter, and after pondering the gifts listed there, mention the names of people your group might know (public or parish figures or members of the group) who do love:

> genuinely
> shrinking from evil and clinging to good
> warmly
> preferring the other to self
> zealously, burning in spirit
> serving the Lord
> rejoicing in hope
> enduring in affliction
> steadfastly continuing in prayer
> sharing the needs of the saints
> practicing hospitality.

Conclude with a prayer of thanksgiving that the Spirit has poured so much love into human hearts.

■ In the first section of his book *Sadhana*, Anthony de Mello, S.J. teaches us how to become more aware of our bodies as a prelude to contemplation. Spend ten minutes of silence in your group sensing your own face, although you can't see or hear it. What is happening on, in, to your chin? your cheek? your eyelid? etc. Then discuss your experience.

Now spend ten minutes concentrated on your own breathing. After five minutes on the experience of breathing itself, breathe God in, God's truth, beauty, love, breathe God in deeply. Breathe out whatever angers you, frightens you,

your pride, your worries, your little greeds. Breathe in God
. . . After the ten minutes, share your feelings with the group.

- Discussion Questions:

For the married: if one of your children claimed to have
the gift of celibacy for the sake of the kingdom, how would
you respond? Why?

For the single: list the pros and cons for marriage and for
celibacy.

For the committed celibate: would you encourage unmarried adult Christians to consider joining with you for mis-
sion/ministry? Why or why not?

- By now your group should know each other quite well.
This exercise asks you to celebrate the gifts of one another.
You might like to set it in the context of a prayer service. Take
a sheet of paper for each member of the group. In silence, look
at someone and remember his or her gifts shared in this group
or gifts you've observed in other situations. List these gifts under the member's name and begin a new sheet for the second
person, etc. Collect all papers for John in one pile, Jean in another, etc. Then give the list of John's gifts to Jean, Jean's gifts
to Joe, etc. Let the list of gifts be read slowly, reverently, so
that Joe is really proclaiming Jean's gifts publicly. At the end
of the proclamation, give the lists to their owners. With some
hymns, psalms and prayers this might be an excellent way to
conclude your group's work. Would that each member would
now gather and lead a new group "on pilgrimage."

For Further Reading

Bonhoeffer, Dietrich. *Life Together.* New York: Harper &
    Row, Publishers, 1954.
    This little classic by the martyr of Nazi Germany focuses

on community, both in family and adult groups. It includes the topics of worship and ministry.

de Mello, Anthony, S.J. *Sadhana: A Way to God.* St. Louis, Missouri: The Institute of Jesuit Sources, 1978.

Duffy, Regis. *Real Presence.* San Francisco: Harper & Row, Publishers, 1982.
This book emphasizes how seriously committed we must be to celebrate the Eucharist. The author particularly throws light on the Corinthian celebration.

Hellwig, Monika. *The Eucharist and the Hunger of the World.* New York: Paulist Press, 1976.

Kelsey, Morton T. *Caring.* New York: Paulist Press, 1981.
So practical and readable.

McNeill, Donald P., Douglas A. Morrison, Henri J.M. Nouwen. *Compassion, a Reflection on the Christian life.* Garden City, New York: Doubleday, 1982.
The call to compassion is the center of Christian life, these three priests assert. The drawings that accompany these powerful essays are themselves almost enough meditation on compassion.

Robinson, John A. T. *The Body.* London: SCM Press Ltd., 1952.
This book by Bishop Robinson is a bit technical. For easier reading, John L. McKenzie summarizes Robinson in the article, "Body" in his Dictionary of the Bible, *New York: Macmillan, 1965. This paperback, one-volume dictionary is worth the group's purchasing if Scripture study/prayer will be pursued.*

Conclusion

I conclude this book, watching the Atlantic at Ocean City, Maryland. It is a winter water and the incoming tide floods the beach beyond its summer boundaries. I hope that this book with its passages for prayer and sharing has flooded you with Spirit. The tides may withdraw again in your life, but I will continue to pray for you, that you may return again and again to the Scriptures themselves to be flooded, lavished, freed for mission and ministry. There is so much more to study, pray, contemplate in the letters of Paul. Even his near contemporaries found him difficult to understand (2 Peter 3:15–16). Today's scholars can argue over every sentence, it seems. I have simply highlighted, in broad strokes, some important experiences of Paul which might affirm or stretch our own religious experience. You can continue that process.

In continuing to study Paul and pray with his letters, we must remember that Paul was responding to particular problems of particular communities. We do not have all his thinking, all his decisions, so we must be careful not to absolutize his partial truth. Rather than setting forth eternal truths and absolute principles, Paul gave us a method for our own theological reflection. He took the tradition he had received, both Jewish tradition and teachings of the Lord and the Christian community, and gave them new meaning by explaining those traditions in reference to the current situations of a particular community of his. He did not substitute new tradition for old torah, new norms for old, but remained flexible, discerning of the Spirit's teaching and moving in Paul's own heart and in the community. We might think of this tentmaker using his tools of trade to stitch new wineskins for the new wine of the risen Lord, and all that the life of that Lord poured out would, could mean for Paul's time, for this community in Greece, for that community in Asia Minor. We need the same openness and freedom as we try to explain the new wine to people of our time, our space.

Thus, I hope I have offered you *some* of the truth of Paul which will be helpful for your (singular and plural) salvation, the only kind of truth which Vatican II says is legitimate to expect from biblical teachings. Indeed, we did not even attend to some very important themes in Paul's experience—for example, the question of the Jews in God's plan. Instead, I did select passages which, hopefully, would nourish more immediately our relationship with God, our prayer.

Of course, the passages in this book are my favorites at this point in my life. I encourage you to work through the letters on your own or in a group to discover your own favorites. One of my assignments to my students is to compose guided prayer questions and comments to help others make the Scripture concrete and contemporary. I urge you to do that for each other in your group, exchanging favorite passages from Paul's letters with some questions and suggestions for prayer. Your group could also continue its life together by creating more group exercises. Another way to study/pray with Paul in a group is to read one verse aloud, pause, reflect and then let anyone who is so moved make an application to his or her personal, parish, or political life. This should be done in a faith-sharing atmosphere without discussion, judgment, or argument so that the group can be enriched by the *variety* of meanings that the group can discover in just one verse. I would recommend the letter to the Ephesians, although probably not written by Paul, as a starting point for further reading, praying and group work. There is much that is "helpful to our salvation" in other letters attributed to Paul, but perhaps none so summarizing of Paul's religious experience and definitely none so poetic, so beautiful as Ephesians.

In conclusion, let me sum up some of Paul's teaching on prayer and offer further reminders and suggestions for "praying always." We can pray always because prayer is God's gift, God's outpouring of the Spirit in our hearts. The Spirit keeps us continually united to God, keeps continually crying from deep within us, "Abba." The Spirit who knows us more intimately than we can ever know ourselves pleads on our behalf, expressing to God for us all those inarticulate groanings, all those only half-conscious desires of our hearts. To pray always means to be in relationship with God always, and that is accomplished always by the Spirit and in Christ.

In Christ we live and move and have our being. The risen Lord can address us as really and as personally as he addressed Paul on the road to Damascus. The Lord initiates all our conscious prayer, and our prayer is response to his word to us in Scripture and in life, his word to us in sin and in grace. Our own words can be response to him. Prayer can be conversation with God, Jesus, the Spirit. This differs from introspection in which we talk to ourselves. Prayer is a dialogue. Not only our words, however, but also our feelings of wonder, love, anger, fear, joy, gratitude, sorrow, etc., and our whole lives can be response to his initiating love.

Because we are so intimately joined with him, the Lord particularly asks us to share his dying and rising. A helpful way to keep that mystery, that invitation before us is to pay attention each evening to the movements or moments of death and resurrection in our daily living. Eventually we may become aware of and consciously share dying or rising with Jesus at the very moment when we are experiencing the anguish or the joy. Notice that this kind of nightly, or even weekly, "examination of conscience" is more biblical, more baptismal, more Christ-centered than examining ourselves for faults and failings. It also serves as a good preparation for celebrating the Eucharist. If we choose to continue examining our lives for sin, however, may I suggest that we examine them for grace as well, so that we can shift the focus to God and keep our self-inspection in perspective.

When we pray, we need to use ever more of our body, *soma*, "the totality of concrete human existence" (McKenzie). Rather than just using our minds and wills, we need to use our memories, imaginations, feelings, intuitions and five senses as often as possible when we pray. The more we involve our whole person in this relationship (prayer), the more we let Jesus take flesh in us. Gradually it will no longer be ourselves who live and work and play and pray but Christ who will live more fully in us (Gal 2:20).

Above all, Paul tells us to be who we are with God who loves us as we are and who gave us the Son when we were yet enemies. There is no need to work for grace—it is freely given. There is no need to achieve God's love—it is already lavished. There is no need to prove our goodness—we are approved and made right with God through Christ Jesus. We have moved along on our pilgrimage. Paul assures us: "I am certain that God will bring to completion the good work which God has begun in you" (Phil 1:6).

For Further Reading

Cardenal, Ernesto. *The Gospel in Solentiname*. (4 vols.) Maryknoll, N.Y.: Orbis Books, 1976.
    *This book uses the technique of line-by-line sharing that

I propose in this chapter. These peasants and fisherfolk of Nic-aragua comment verse by verse on Gospel passages with a profound wisdom derived from their lived experience of God in the midst of their poverty.

The Letter to the Ephesians from the New Testament.